REVIVING AMERICA

ALSO BY STEVE FORBES

*Money: How the Destruction of the Dollar Threatens
the Global Economy—and What We Can Do About It*
(and Elizabeth Ames)

*How Capitalism Will Save Us: Why Free People and
Free Markets Are the Best Answer in Today's Economy*
(and Elizabeth Ames)

*Freedom Manifesto: Why Free Markets Are
Moral and Big Government Isn't*
(and Elizabeth Ames)

Flat Tax Revolution: Using a Postcard to Abolish the IRS

A New Birth of Freedom: Vision for America

*Power Ambition Glory: The Stunning Parallels
Between Great Leaders of the Ancient World
and Today . . . and the Lessons You Can Learn*
(and John Prevas)

REVIVING AMERICA

How Repealing Obamacare,
Replacing the Tax Code,
and Reforming the Fed will
Restore Hope and Prosperity

Steve Forbes
Elizabeth Ames

New York Chicago San Francisco Athens London
Madrid Mexico City Milan New Delhi
Singapore Sydney Toronto

1 2 3 4 5 6 7 8 9 0   DOC/DOC   1 2 1 0 9 8 7 6 5

ISBN   978-1-259-64112-1
MHID   1-259-64112-0

e-ISBN   978-1-259-64113-8
e-MHID   1-259-64113-9

McGraw-Hill Education books are available at special quantity discounts to use as premiums and sales promotions or for use in corporate training programs. To contact a representative, please visit the Contact Us pages at www.mhprofessional.com.

To the American nation,
which remains, in Lincoln's words,
"the last best hope of earth."

Contents

Acknowledgments

Many people helped make this book possible. Bill Dal Col, who heads up Potomac Communication Strategies and did a superb job in managing Steve's presidential bids despite a less than perfect candidate, strongly urged several months ago that Steve do a book on the critical issues the country faces and get it out in time to help influence the debate for the 2016 election cycle. Knox Huston, our editor at McGraw-Hill, loved that idea and promised to move Heaven and Earth to speed up the normal book publishing process. He delivered. Peter McCurdy at McGraw-Hill helped make possible this minor miracle. We also thank our agent, Jim Hornfischer, for his encouragement and advice.

Our thanks go to Derek Sarley, Stuart Spooner, and Nathan Burchfiel for their timely research on the tax section of this book. We could not have completed this project without the excellent contributions of Elizabeth Gravitt, Akil Alleyne, Nicole Hungerford, Sue Radlauer, Keith Farrell, Ryan Hagemann, and Lamont Wood.

We also thank Bob Mansfield and David Lada for their help on the graphs.

This book owes a debt to some the nation's leading free market thinkers in the fields of healthcare, taxes, and monetary policy. Among them: the brilliant Nathan Lewis, the foremost expert on gold. His books *Gold: The Once and Future Money* and *Gold: The Monetary Polaris* are required reading for anyone interested in gaining a serious understanding of this crucial subject. David Malpass is just about the only economist of note who has correctly diagnosed the disastrous results of the Federal Reserve's experiments with quantitative easing, zero interest rates, and regulatory overkill. We are very grateful for his insights.

Dan Mitchell's knowledge of and enthusiasm for the Flat Tax remains unparalleled.

Thankfully, on the critical subject of healthcare there are growing number of people who truly "get" what ails this most personal of endeavors, that is, the lack of free markets. Among those who provided information and analyses were Merrill Matthews and Grace-Marie Turner. Although they bear absolutely no responsibility whatsoever for what we wrote on healthcare, the writings of and conversations with Matthew Herper and Avik Roy at *Forbes* were always stimulating and informed.

We are also very grateful to Mia Carbonell, Nina LaFrance, Jessica Feintisch, Coates Bateman, and Christina Vega at *Forbes* and Elena Christie and Courtney Fischer at McGraw-Hill for their wonderful work on marketing and promotion.

We would also like to thank Alexander McCobin, Frederik Roeder, and Casey Given at Students for Liberty for their excellent recommendations and support, not to mention their tireless efforts around the world on behalf of free people and free markets.

Finally, Steve could not even begin to function without the help of associates Jackie DeMaria, Rebecca Tapio, and Merrill Vaughan.

Needless to say, without the understanding and encouragement of family, a project like this would be well nigh impossible. A heartfelt thank you to Sabina, Steve's wife, and their five daughters, Sabina, Roberta, Catherine, Moira, and Elizabeth. In particular Sabina, Catherine, and Moira helped their father cope with his battles with laptops, iPads, and iPhones.

Introduction

*H*OW DO WE REVIVE AMERICA? BOTH LEFT AND RIGHT agree the nation has lost its way. The Great Recession that followed the historic financial meltdown of the mid-2000s officially ended in 2009. But the recovery is the weakest ever from a major downturn—so weak, in fact, that some 60% of Americans feel that the economy is still in decline.

Poll after poll shows that people have lost faith in the system. This national funk is explained by the numbers. Since 2009 Americans have seen a sharp decline in real incomes. The biggest drop has been experienced by the bottom 20% of income earners. [See chart.]

Decline in Real Wages, 2009 to 2014

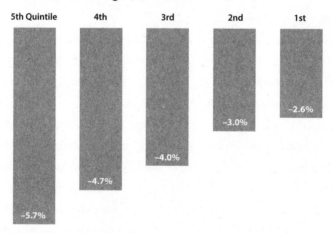

Source: NELP analysis of May 2009 and 2014 Occupational Employment Statistics.

1

Within the past couple of years, the employment picture has improved, but the labor participation rate—which reflects the number of people who have dropped out of the workforce—is the lowest in decades.

More and more adults are concluding that their children and grandchildren won't do as well as they did and will face a lower standard of living. With the American dream of upward mobility appearing to fade, many wonder whether America's days as the optimistic, can-do land of opportunity are over. Yet the Washington politicians appear clueless about what needs to be done.

The policies of Barack Obama, the president who was supposed to bring us "hope and change," have given us a disheartened, divided America. Public anger has resulted in riots and demonstrations on a scale not seen in this country since the 1960s and early 1970s. In this ugly atmosphere, political sniping and scapegoating are increasingly taking the place of rational public discourse. People are directing their rage towards immigrants, bankers, the "rich," "idlers" content to live off government handouts—and even the police.

Things are even worse abroad. Malignant forces, especially Islamic fanatics, grow in strength, emboldened by an America that seems to have abandoned its role as the leader of the Free World. Russian dictator Vladimir Putin commits aggression against Ukraine, a sovereign nation, while also threatening other neighbors and openly challenging the U.S. in the Mideast and the Arctic. Elsewhere, China brazenly flexes its muscles and taunts the U.S. by sending naval vessels to the edge of U.S. waters. Constructing man-made islands in a disputed area of the South China Sea, its actions underscore a global perception of the U.S. as a declining power.

Our nation seems mired in a malaise that evokes comparisons with the 1970s. Is this uncertain, polarized and economically stagnant America really, to use a favorite term of political elites, "the new normal"? The answer is a most emphatic *No*.

With the courage and the leadership to enact the right policies, this country can rebound—and rebound quickly. This book lays out the bold actions necessary for an American Revival that will restore faith in our nation as the land of opportunity and hope.

As this is being written, we are entering the 2016 election season. Politicians are floating ideas for curing our ailing country. Some of them have merit. But three crucial areas must come first in any program of meaningful reform: healthcare, taxes, and monetary policy. Each is a source of major dysfunction that must be addressed if we are to finally get the nation back on track.

That's why reviving America must start with what we're calling The Big Three Reforms. Three big reforms—to healthcare, taxes, and money. Get these things right and the country will make a quick and dramatic turnaround that will rival and indeed exceed the great comeback America achieved under the presidency of Ronald Reagan in the early 1980s.

So our book is divided into three parts: Part One discusses healthcare, which makes up almost 20% of our economy. The solution here is not only to repeal Obamacare. We must also address fundamental problems predating Obamacare that created the political environment that gave us that terrible law. Part One explains how decades of government regulation have all but destroyed normal markets in both healthcare and insurance. The left likes to blame what's ailing healthcare on "greed" and "free markets." But the problem is the opposite: too much government and too little economic freedom. Healthcare is one of the country's two most heavily regulated sectors. (The other—no surprise—is finance, another troubled area of the economy.)

What's actually driving today's rising healthcare prices is our government-dominated "third-party payer" system, whereby employers, government, private insurers—but not the patient— are the ones that pay for healthcare. The market is therefore tailored to their needs and not to yours as the healthcare consumer.

To achieve meaningful reform, this system—a distortion brought about by World War II regulations and a 1954 change in our tax law—must be overhauled. Doing so would bring down today's spiraling healthcare costs and unleash a new era of innovation that would truly make both insurance and care more available and affordable.

Part Two looks at the federal income tax code, that growing monster sapping America's vitality. With its tangle of tax brackets and regulatory complexities, our current system is a major barrier to progress. It has helped create an IRS that, in criminal fashion, threatens our very liberties.

This book sets forth a simple and drastic solution: throw out the income tax code and replace it with a simple Flat Tax allowing you to literally fill out your entire tax return on a single sheet of paper—or with a few keystrokes on your computer.

This reform may sound radical. But as we explain in Part Two, a Flat Tax is easy to adopt and has turned around numerous economies. Unlike other proposals such as the Fair Tax, the Flat Tax has a track record. *It really works.*

Part Three looks at monetary policy, specifically the need to drastically reform the Federal Reserve System. The effects of the Fed's fluctuating U.S. dollar—whose value rises and falls based on the whims of central bankers—get scant attention from Washington politicians. But this system must change if we are to once more enjoy true prosperity. If we don't get monetary policy right, we will never realize the full potential of the American economy.

The Fed's mistakes not only endanger the U.S. but also economies around the world. Just look at the daily headlines about the currency turmoil afflicting Europe, Japan, Brazil, Indonesia (home to the world's largest population of Muslims), South Africa, and others.

Part Three presents the one real solution to today's out-of-control central bank: a return to a monetary system based on a stable dollar whose value is linked to gold. America had a gold standard for most of its history. It helped our economy become the greatest in the world, and it can do so again—if the politicians let it.

Many people today are too young to remember that America also faced a similar period of self-doubt and malaise during the decade of the seventies. Then, as now, many people here and abroad concluded we were a fading power whose best days were over. Campaigning for president, former California governor Ronald Reagan combined withering criticisms of his opponent, the hapless incumbent president Jimmy Carter, with a positive program to revive this country. Most prominent among his proposals was a 30% cut in income tax rates for everyone. Reagan promised to end the seemingly incurable inflation that was sapping the economy and the nation's morale. He also proposed the biggest peacetime military buildup ever as a means to rebuild our armed forces, along with a vigorous foreign policy to turn back the seemingly unstoppable advances of our longtime Cold War adversary, the Soviet Union.

Experts and most political pundits thought his ideas preposterous. But Reagan was right. His landslide victory in 1980 provided the mandate to enact most of his program. Stabilizing the dollar, he killed debilitating inflation once and for all. His massive income tax cuts and other pro-growth initiatives swiftly turned the economy around. Thanks to Reagan, the U.S. for more than three decades led the world in growth and innovation. Reagan-era reforms helped encourage the rise of Silicon Valley, whose cutting-edge technologies have transformed not only the U.S. but also the global economy.

Along with demonstrating the power of free markets to revitalize a nation, Reagan showed the importance of domestic economic strength for leadership abroad. A decade after his ascendency to the White House, the Soviet Union lay in tatters and had ceased to exist.

If we are to avoid a miserable future in an increasingly chaotic world, America must again experience the kind of resurgence that took place after World War II and again in the 1980s. We *can* achieve a comparable comeback—if we do the right things. To bring about a genuine revival in the 21st century, the U.S. must put in place a Reaganite program of reform that removes the shackles of government and unleashes the brainpower and resources of the American people.

You may ask why we didn't devote a section to the crisis of entitlements, specifically Social Security, Medicare, and Medicaid. Their unfunded liabilities now run into the tens of *trillions* of dollars. Some may also wonder why we're not addressing the abuses of out-of-control agencies like the EPA and others.

The answer is *first things first*. The proposals in this book will also make it far easier to enact those subsequent reforms. Overhauling the healthcare system, for example, will change Medicare and Medicaid by scaling back the liabilities of those giant programs. The roaring economy—and tax revenues—to result from our Big Three Reforms will also mean the future cost burden of Social Security will be sharply reduced. Ultimately, the long-term answer for Social Security is to bring in personal accounts for younger people. Much is at stake, and not just for America. We too often fail to recognize the dangerous global consequences of domestic weakness. We saw this in the 1930s.

Weakened by the Great Depression, Britain and France pursued passive foreign policies in the face of Nazi Germany, Imperial Japan, and fascist Italy. The U.S. retreated into isolationism. The dictatorships struck observers as being purposeful and strong while the democracies were listless, demoralized, and corrupt. The blunt truth is that, if there had been no Great Depression, there would have been no Nazi Revolution (the Nazis received only 2% of the vote in 1928). If there had been no Nazi Revolution, there would have been no World War II.

With today's rise of extremism abroad and, to a lesser extent, at home, it is vital that we rediscover the principles of economic freedom that brought about the American Revival under Ronald Reagan. They are the principles of the Founders who built the American republic: an unshakeable faith in a society based on free people and free markets, equal opportunity (not equal outcome), property rights, and the rule of law. These tenets must be the basis of any and all reforms. We must start by reforming healthcare, taxes, and money. Just how do we propose to do this? To get the answers, read on . . .

PART ONE

REPEAL OBAMACARE:
Lower Costs and Improve Care by Putting Patients and Their Doctors in Charge

CHAPTER 1

Why Healthcare Today
Is Such a Mess

W E'VE PUT HEALTHCARE AT THE TOP OF OUR LIST OF reforms because it is uniquely personal. All of us at various points in our lives need medical care. The debate over the problems in healthcare thus evokes powerful emotions. If there's one thing that the American people agree upon, it's that the system is a mess. Nearly everyone has a complaint—from long waits for doctors, to the difficulty in getting coverage for an expensive, much-needed drug, to a rigid market for health insurance with few choices and ever-increasing premiums. And let's not forget increasingly cold and impersonal hospitals with rotating shifts of doctors and nurses. Along with the challenges of dealing with illness, patients and their loved ones often have to fight a Kafkaesque hospital bureaucracy to receive tests and treatments.

The Affordable Care Act (that is, Obamacare) was intended to be the answer to what ails healthcare. Yet it did anything but fix these problems. Instead, as we discuss in the next chapter, the law has in fact made them many times worse.

The troubles in healthcare have long been blamed on "free markets"—i.e., insurance companies, doctors, drug companies and hospitals whose greatest concern, supposedly, is making money. Leading up to the passage of Obamacare, you may remember countless stories of heartless, "greedy" insurers denying coverage to sick patients. One such story in *Time* magazine recounted the case of a man who lost his insurance just before he was to get an expensive treatment for lymphoma and another of a woman who had to fight to keep her coverage on the eve of a double mastectomy.

Another frequently cited symptom of America's health-care disaster: out-of-control costs throughout the system. In his now-classic book *Catastrophic Care: Why Everything We Think We Know about Health Care Is Wrong*, David Goldhill adds up what a typical American will pay for medical care during a life-time. He tallies not just the direct, but the indirect costs: insurance co-pays and deductibles; out-of-pocket expenses not covered by insurance; Medicare taxes deducted from our paychecks; state and federal taxes paid for the out-of-control costs of Medicaid. He also includes the hit to our salaries from employers who divert resources to pay for costly employer-provided health insurance.

Total tab? A staggering $1.9 million.

But, according to the "experts," free market "greed" is not the only culprit. Also blamed: *Too much demand!* You'll hear the familiar wail from politicians and pundits: What are we going to do about all those aging Baby Boomers flooding the market for healthcare and overusing the system? *We must find a way to stop so much healthcare spending!*

The real problem with healthcare is these grossly misguided perceptions that have given us destructive public policies. Our healthcare system is like a patient who has been misdiagnosed and treated time and again with the wrong medicine. What happens? He just keeps getting sicker.

Free markets haven't produced the high prices and scarcity plaguing healthcare. The real cause: government controls that have been in place for decades. Healthcare is the most heavily regulated sector of our economy and had been long before Obamacare.

American healthcare may not be government-controlled like Britain's National Health Service. In the U.S. there are private-sector doctors and drug companies and even scattered pockets of free markets here and there. That is why we still produce more new drugs and medical devices than the rest of the world. But overall, free markets are largely absent from a sector that represents 18% of our economy.

Six decades of growing government involvement has grossly distorted the healthcare system. The result is that you, the patient, are no longer the real customer in this artificially configured market. Third parties are insurers, government, hospitals, and employers. For all the palaver to the contrary, patients are generally at the bottom of this food chain. One small example: not even the crummiest motel would put you in a room with other guests as hospitals do with sick people. Nor would they dare give you the kind of gowns provided by most hospitals and clinics.

After all, why should hospitals care about such niceties? You're not paying the bill. An angry hotel customer can take his business elsewhere and warn friends and family to stay away. But you have no such leverage as a hospital patient. That's not just because you're sick but also because you're not controlling the healthcare dollar. Your insurer is.

But the lack of free markets is more than a matter of hospital gowns. Each year tens of thousands of patients die from secondary infections acquired in the course of a hospital stay. This is scandalous. Imagine what the public reaction would be to a restaurant chain that caused even a handful of people to die from food poisoning. There would be angry demands for investigations into sanitary conditions and practices. Not so with hospitals because they're not seen as being directly accountable to patients.

Then there's the matter of prices. If you go to a hospital or clinic and ask in advance what your treatment is going to cost, you'll get a very strange look. Why would you want to know the price? What's it to you? Your insurer or the government will deal with that. All you should care about is what your out-of-pocket costs will be.

With every other product or service, the first thing we want to know is: What does it cost? In other words, in healthcare today, there is a profound disconnect between providers and consumers, or in this case, patients.

Hospitals know who their *real* customers are: insurers and Big Government. Insurers, meanwhile, know that their critical relationships are with employers, hospital chains, and Big Government. Your employer's deals are with insurers. The biggest companies can make special arrangements for pricing and access with hospitals and specialized clinics. You, the patient, are the supposed beneficiary of these relationships. But the reality is that you are largely a powerless bystander. Meanwhile, your out-of-pocket expenses—co-pays, deductibles, gaps in traditional Medicare coverage, and the like—are going up and up.

This is true of both private and government insurance. Medicare was created to rescue seniors on fixed incomes from the ever-increasing cost of medical care in old age. That hasn't happened. Instead, seniors today spend a greater proportion of their retirement income on healthcare than their forebears did before Medicare was created in 1965.

Another indicator of this dysfunctional market: the very fact that healthcare demand is considered a *crisis*. In just about every other sector of the economy, increased demand is viewed as an *opportunity*. No one complains of a crisis, for example, when a mobile device flies off store shelves—or when automakers are working overtime to keep up with orders for cars and trucks. Quite the contrary: You'd see awe-struck articles in business publications about how everyone wants that hot new smartphone. Or that GM, Ford, or Nissan can't keep up with demand for their vehicles. In normal free markets, demand for autos, cell phones, and other products is something to be *celebrated*.

That's precisely our point: We don't have real free markets in healthcare.

Critics' usual response: you can't have free markets because healthcare is "different." This skepticism is summed up by the question: How can you comparison shop for emergency rooms when you're in an ambulance suffering a heart attack? You can't be sure when you'll need medical treatment. And you can't predict what kind of insurance coverage you need. And there's all that expensive technology.

In fact, most medical care is not of an emergency nature, and the insurance that pays for your care is not bought when you're in an ambulance. Free markets exist for many products and services that have the same "problems" as healthcare—for instance, computers (like healthcare, advanced and often expensive technology) and auto insurance (unpredictability). Yet these markets work. How many people have trouble finding affordable computers, phones, cars, or clothes? Have you ever heard anyone in this country talk about a *cell phone crisis?* The only crises we may have heard about have been the result of *too many* cell phones, and people using them at the wrong time—in theaters or texting while driving. But no one's demanding an Obamacare act for cell phones.

Few people fully appreciate the insidiousness of the third-party payer system and how it has distorted the delivery of healthcare. In a normal market, competitors vie for the business of consumers. Some may fail. But the winners do more than cash in. Their bestselling products and services lift up the rest of the market. Apple's success with the iPhone caused companies like Samsung to rush in with their own, similar offerings. When this happens, prices come down and standards are raised for all consumers.

With its lack of upfront consumer pricing that you see before you buy, the third-party payer system preempts this process and keeps healthcare services from advancing and improving. Kaiser Permanente, the Geisinger Health System, and a handful of other institutions have been lauded for practicing truly integrated medicine instead of the increasingly silo-ed approach of most hospitals, where specialists never seem to talk to one another.   Yet third-party reimbursement rates at these institutions can be the same as at hospitals with far inferior results. Reimbursements depend not on performance but rather on how hospitals negotiate with insurers.

What this means is that there's no market mechanism—i.e., higher profits—to show Geisinger and Kaiser Permanente's "best practices" are considered desirable. So they're less likely to be widely adopted by other healthcare providers—the way, say, a terrific new computer technology would spread and become an industry standard. In true free markets, entrepreneurs would be rapidly figuring out how to cash in by topping what Geisinger and Kaiser offer, just as companies like Samsung quickly leapt at the huge market Apple had pioneered with the iPhone and iPad with products that were cheaper or offered allegedly better features.

The ultimate third-party system, of course, was the Soviet Union, where the consumer had no market power. Products were shoddy and central planners couldn't even begin to match the cornucopia of high-tech breakthroughs coming from the U.S. and other nations with open markets.

The powerful influence of giant government insurers Medicare and Medicaid is another reason for the bureaucratization of healthcare. Their reimbursement policies, which set the agenda for private insurers, constrain care and innovation.

For example, why have doctors been so slow to make use of computers and the Internet, things commonly used by corporate America, in the day-to-day practice of medicine? The explanation is not simply, as some have observed, that doctors tend to be reluctant to change. A reason widely overlooked is that Medicare doesn't reimburse for such tools because they weren't used back in 1965.

Obamacare has attempted to modernize medical offices by compelling doctors to computerize medical records. But, as we discuss in the next chapter, it is doing so with an overly heavy hand that is deepening problems in healthcare and further impeding the practice of medicine.

Big Government advocates hate to admit this, but in a normal free market, the prevailing trend is for the quality of products and services to keep improving and for prices to go *down*, not up. Compare a television set of 10 years ago with the typical widescreen set today. The quality has tremendously improved and the price has plummeted to a fraction of what it was.

Free markets will always turn scarcity into abundance. Back in the early 1900s, an automobile cost today's equivalent of some $125,000. Along came Henry Ford, who, along with a gifted group of engineers, ultimately created the moving assembly line, which drastically cut costs and vastly increased output. Result: a toy for the rich became something every working person could afford.

This doesn't happen in healthcare because prices aren't set by countless providers rushing in to meet demand. Instead, costs are determined based on the needs and wants of a handful of big government and corporate entities with fat checkbooks.

In addition to third-party pay, another factor driving healthcare costs is the sheer volume of government rules and regulations. This had been the case long before Obamacare. In each state, for example, insurers have been governed by different coverage mandates requiring that they reimburse just about every conceivable expense—whether people needed or wanted this or not.

Thanks to these state regulations, the healthcare coverage we have today is not really traditional insurance, which is supposed to cover big, unforeseeable risks. No one expects their homeowners insurance, for instance, to reimburse for a broken coffee mug, mowing the lawn, trimming the trees, or filling up the heating oil tank. Motorists don't file claims for gas fill-ups or car washes. Imagine how high your auto insurance premium would be if Geico or Liberty Mutual reimbursed for every tank of gasoline.

The sky-rocketing health insurance premiums of the past decade—which gave rise to the public indignation that brought about Obamacare—are largely the result of these costly insurance regulations driving smaller insurance companies out of the market. Less competition inevitably leads to higher prices. In 2009, then senior White House advisor David Axelrod himself admitted to CNN's Wolf Blitzer that, "in many states in this country, there is one insurer that dominates the entire market. In Alabama, one insurer dominates 87%. In North Dakota, there's one insurer that dominates the market almost completely." Blitzer responded with a question asked today by many who want to replace Obamacare: "Why not break down the state barriers and let all of these insurance companies compete nationally, without having to simply focus in on a state-by-state basis?"

Why not, indeed?

A 2014 report released by the American Medical Association (AMA) found that 72% of some 388 metropolitan insurance markets lacked industry competition and were "highly concentrated."

But insurance regulations are only part of this mess. Government constraints on what doctors and hospitals can and cannot do are worthy of Soviet-era central planning. Among the worst are so-called "certificate-of-need" laws. In more than half the states in the U.S., anyone who wants to build a new hospital, a nursing home, a burn unit—or countless other types of facilities—must obtain a certificate of need. Some states have declared moratoria on certain facilities. In 2014, the state of Delaware declared that no additional hospitals offering medical/surgical or obstetrical beds were to be built. Louisiana has called a halt to building long-term care nursing facilities. *But what if people need them?*

Samsung is not required to obtain a "certificate of need" to compete with Apple. Dunkin' Donuts does not apply for a certificate of need to set up shop near Starbucks. That gets to our point about certificates of need: *they're not needed.*

Doing away with certificates of need and other anticompetitive regulations would accelerate the proliferation of alternative delivery systems such as walk-in clinics and centers that could provide vital services to people at lower cost. Some have already been launched by major retailers. For example, CVS Pharmacy offers MinuteClinics, where nurse practitioners diagnose and treat common family illnesses, like strep throat and bladder infections. Without regulatory barriers it would be easier for a CVS or a Walgreens—or some other provider—to bring innovations and low prices to other areas of healthcare.

And we haven't yet mentioned the countless rules and regulations impeding *existing* healthcare providers. A medium-sized acute care facility in San Diego, California, was found to be accountable to 39 governmental agencies and seven non-governmental bodies. There were 65 separate reports that it had to file with these organizations, which translated to roughly one report for every four beds. Achieving "compliance" required highly trained, expensive hospital personnel each and every day to record detailed information.

And that's just one hospital. The story is the same throughout the system. To get a single drug approved by the Food and Drug Administration, for example, takes about 10 years. The entire process can cost more than $2 billion. Back in 2004, a groundbreaking study by Duke University's Christopher Conover found that government regulation of the medical sector—including regulation of medical practitioners and facilities, health insurance, drugs, and medical devices—cost the economy between $256 billion and

$339.2 billion or more per year. The net burden of such regulation added up to "a $169 billion hidden tax."

Health insurance would be many times cheaper—and you'd get more for your dollar—if you, the patient, paid for it and not big third-party corporations and government. The magic of consumerism works even in the technologically advanced field of medical care.

In the small pockets of healthcare that are consumer-driven markets, prices have steadily come down and service has improved. One example: Lasik surgery to correct vision. Millions have had the procedure done so they don't have to wear glasses or contact lenses. Insurance rarely covers this operation and so there is not the normal disconnect between provider and customer. Providers thus have to attract consumers—i.e., you the patient—by improving results and making more surgery affordable. The procedure today costs *less* than it did a decade ago. *Forbes* magazine publisher Rich Karlgaard paid $5,000 for Lasik in the early part of the last decade. He recently observed that he could probably have the same operation done for $2,500 today and get an even better result.

Cosmetic surgery is another specialty not covered by insurance. Demand has grown more than six-fold in the last two decades, and there have been enormous technological breakthroughs. But cosmetic surgery has not experienced the inflation that has wracked the rest of the medical field. And as anyone can see from the popular media—or from casual observation—it's widely and easily available to just about anyone who wants it.

Advocates of government healthcare hate the idea of consumers paying for their own care or insurance. But a consumer-driven market is the only way to achieve their objectives of lowering costs and spending. The National Bureau of Economic Research (NBER) in March 2015 studied the impact of what are called consumer-directed health plans (CDHPs) over a three-year period. These employer-provided policies combine high deductibles with health saving accounts (HSAs). For those who may not be familiar with them, an HSA is a tax-free IRA-like account, which you can get from your employer to pay for routine healthcare expenses. The great virtue of these is that, if you save money on generic drugs or doctor visits, you keep the money you save, not your employer or the government. What you save rolls over into the following year and collects interest.

What impact have these consumer-driven plans had on spending? According to the NBER's study, "Spending is reduced for those in firms offering CDHPs. . . . The reductions are driven by spending decreases in outpatient care and pharmaceuticals, with no evidence of increases in emergency department or inpatient care." These findings are a stunning rebuke to Big Government types who insist that you can't reduce healthcare costs without government cost controls and rationing.

You may be wondering: If consumer-driven markets are the best solution for healthcare, then why don't we currently have them? Today's system is the accidental outgrowth of government wage-and-price controls put in place during World War II. Uncle Sam wanted to keep companies from raising wages—and prices— as a result of the domestic labor shortage arising from millions of Americans going into the military. Employers prevented from enticing workers with higher salaries turned to offering fringe benefits—like health insurance.

After the war, Washington formally allowed employers to treat these insurance outlays as a tax-deductible expense while not treating them as taxable income for workers. This institutionalized the third-party pay system. The government's tax incentives encouraged employers to pay for their worker's health insurance. The consequence was that employees were insulated from the cost of coverage and medical care.

In the 1960s, the market distortions of third-party pay were vastly amplified by the establishment of Medicare and Medicaid, the two giant government insurers. Market forces were prevented from operating in what is probably the largest segment of the healthcare market—providers to the poor and the elderly.

Over the years employees have been asked to pay more for their own healthcare through higher co-pays and deductibles. Yet people have remained largely insulated from the true cost of healthcare. We will see in the next chapter how the added federal restraints of Obamacare made a bad situation dramatically worse. The law, however, has had one unintended positive effect: it has inadvertently created a bigger consumer market, thanks to the immense deductibles of the government-subsidized plans on Obamacare exchanges.

After recovering from the sticker shock of high deductibles, millions of Americans are paying for many expenses out of pocket and becoming more cost-conscious healthcare consumers. Thus, Barack Obama, who devoutly wishes for a truly socialist, single-payer system, has been unintentionally paving the way for free market reform. He's cultivating a greater acceptance among Americans for paying for healthcare in a consumer-driven market.

CHAPTER 2

How Obamacare
Made the Situation Worse
and Not Better

THE 2010 PASSAGE OF THE PATIENT PROTECTION AND Affordable Care Act (also known as Obamacare) was supposed to fix the problems in healthcare. But like so many politicized government interventions, it has made them many, many times worse. Obamacare has subjected a system bogged down by decades of overregulation to a tangle of new constraints. The result has been the worst of all worlds—costs that have only continued to rise, as the quality and availability of medical care declines.

Remember former Democratic Speaker of the House Nancy Pelosi's now-infamous insistence that we had to pass Obamacare to know what's in it? Had Pelosi herself known what was in this miserable law, and the impact it would have on her job and those of her fellow Democrats, she might not have been so arrogant. Public rage over its passage led to some 63 House members losing their seats in the 2010 election, causing Pelosi to lose her job as Speaker. And half of the Senators who voted for the bill subsequently also lost their jobs.

Supporters insisted Obamacare would make healthcare and insurance more available and affordable. They sold it as the answer to the supposed problem of the 46 million people in the U.S. who were uninsured. Put aside the fact that many of the uninsured were young people who did not want health insurance. Whatever the extent of that problem, Obamacare has proven a toxic response that has only exacerbated the problems in healthcare. This monstrous legislation was based on the mistaken notion that politicians can solve problems by imposing top-down central planning "solutions" on a healthcare market of hundreds of millions of people.

We all know the big headline-making stories: the failure of the billion-dollar federal website HealthCare.gov to function and the additional failures of state insurance exchanges. And then there's the notorious promise, "if you like your health care plan you can keep your health care plan," a deliberate deception on the part of the president and Obamacare advocates in the administration. Millions of people had to scramble to get coverage after being kicked off "non-compliant" insurance plans before the law entirely took effect.

But wait, there's more: increased premiums for millions of Americans at almost every income level; a tsunami of regulation and bureaucracy that has lowered the quality and availability of care for patients covered both by government (Medicare and Medicaid) and private insurance plans; and also a growing shortage of doctors leaving the profession or joining group practices because they no longer can make a living under Obamacare's paltry reimbursements.

The law has also failed in its mission to make healthcare more "affordable." Its health insurance exchanges may provide lots of subsidies to pay premiums, but they don't cover the huge deductibles in most of these policies. Worse still, Obamacare has not stemmed rising prices for medical services. Experts, including Sally Pipes and Scott Gottlieb, have pointed out on Forbes.com that the annual rise in the cost of health services has increased from less than 4% a year to almost 6% and that this climb is just beginning.

In addition, the law's micromanaging rules and levies—like the infamous tax on medical devices—have impeded medical innovation. And then there is the damage to the economy: Obamacare's employer mandate, requiring that companies with over 50 employees pay for healthcare, discourages the creation of full-time jobs and the growth of entrepreneurial businesses. The costs and uncertainty created by Obamacare have been widely—and rightly—blamed as a crucial factor in the slow recovery.

Five years after the passage of this monster, opinion polls show that the law continues to be unpopular. Most people believe it has failed to change healthcare for the better. A 2014 Washington Post–ABC News survey of 1,000 adults showed that the greatest number of those surveyed, 44%, felt the healthcare system as a whole had gotten worse since the passage of Obamacare.

Meanwhile, as for their own personal care, only 14% believed it had gotten better, while some 29% also reported that their healthcare had gotten worse; 53% said it has remained the same. Hardly an accomplishment worth the $2.7 trillion that the law is expected to cost in the next 10 years.

What about those articles you occasionally see in the liberal media claiming that the law is a success because more people now have health insurance? The media's Obamacare cheerleaders ignore the fact that much of the new coverage is coming not from exchange-based plans but through Medicaid—hardly known as a provider of high-quality care. Analyst Scott Atlas cites a 2014 study that found that "an estimated 71% of the new insurance arises through Medicaid." Which means many of these new Obamacare recipients will have a rough time finding a doctor. The Physicians Foundation's *2014 Survey of America's Physicians* reports that 38% of physicians limit the number of Medicaid patients they'll treat or refuse them outright.

Healthcare analyst John Graham of the National Center for Policy Analysis similarly says the government's upbeat numbers are misleading:

> The uninsured dropped by 7.9 percentage points, but those who lacked a personal physician dropped only 3.5 percentage points. In other words, 56 percent of those who got insurance under Obamacare still lack access to a personal physician. With respect to Medicaid, it was worse. The number of Medicaid dependents increased 5.2 percentage points but the number lacking a personal physician only dropped 1.8 percentage points. That means 65 percent of those newly enrolled in Medicaid still lack a personal physician. That does not look like success to me. It looks like spending a whole lot of money for little result.

Obamacare has only exacerbated the distortions and unintended consequences of our government-dominated, third-party payer system—which is why it hasn't worked. Below, some more reasons why people hate this law.

A Decline in the Availability and Quality of Care

Obamacare has increased pressure on doctors and insurers to control costs—at the expense of patients whose needs are the lowest priority.

Forbes contributor Paul Hsieh and others have pointed out that Obamacare in various ways is creating incentives to control healthcare costs by "*undertreatment* rather than overtreatment." The healthcare advisory firm Avalere found that Bronze plans offered on the health insurance exchanges created by the Affordable Care Act include 34% fewer providers than the average commercial plan offered outside the exchange.

Patients on Obamacare plans are often shocked to discover that their new government-approved insurance is based on "narrow networks" of doctors and hospitals. Some on these plans have had to travel considerable distances to see those physicians. One colon cancer survivor in Oklahoma discovered she had to drive 400 miles to see the nearest doctor covered under her plan. When she called the Obamacare exchange to complain, the representative told her they receive calls like this "every day."

Patients are also running up against new, rigid bureaucratic diktats, regulations intended to control costs by restricting care. Such rules are overriding the patient care decisions of individual physicians—such as when to admit a patient to a hospital.

Frank Alfisi, a 73-year-old retired produce seller, met his son at a Long Island emergency room. The elder Alfisi had missed a dialysis session after a brief bout with a stomach virus. His blood pressure was dangerously high and he desperately needed dialysis. Despite his condition, he was forced to wait for hours. Finally, the ER doctor informed the family that, while he personally agreed that Alfisi needed dialysis, the hospital could not provide it because, as his daughter later wrote, "it's only covered for inpatients and they could not admit my father as an inpatient because his condition did not meet the new Medicare insurance standards for admission."

The problem was a new Obamacare directive known as the "Two Midnight Rule," which dictates that Medicare does not cover hospital stays of only one night. To comply with the rule, the hospital had to subject Alfisi to a battery of tests to come up with a diagnosis that would enable him to be admitted. The delay in getting care caused his health to spiral dramatically downward. He died two months later. When Alfisi's daughter Amy told one of her father's physicians about his ordeal, the doctor replied, "You can thank Mr. Obama for this."

Obamacare is also hurting patients by squeezing out your personal physician. Instead, "physician extenders" who are not M.D.s, are increasingly administering care. If you are admitted to the hospital, it is also more difficult for your long-term doctor to remain in control of your care. Your case is instead likely to be turned over to a succession of "hospitalists," doctors who are shift workers who know little or nothing about your medical history and who must quickly get up to speed. The actress Janine Turner said that when her father was admitted to the hospital:

> The assigned "hospitalists"—there were different hospitalists every day—started playing Russian roulette with my father's medications for no apparent reason. Trying to talk to one of his hospitalists was impossible, and one hospitalist didn't know what the other hospitalist was doing—which resulted in conflicting messages and careless care.
>
> One of the hospitalists needlessly prescribed a very risky pain medication (especially risky for an elderly man with an extensive and complex medical history) for an ache that was nominal. None of his personal physicians, who knew of his benign aches, ever prescribed this medication because they knew the potential side effects were severe and potentially hazardous. The ends did not justify the means. Two weeks later my father was dead.

These two examples are about seniors and that's no accident. The dirty little secret of Obamacare is that its cost control measures often end up, in one way or another, limiting care of the elderly, who need it most.

In 2015, Medicare announced that it would pay for end-of-life counseling. Healthcare policy analyst Betsy McCaughey writes ruefully, "It's being sold as 'death with dignity,' but it's more like dying for dollars. Seniors are pressured to forego life-sustaining procedures to go into hospice." Unless we return control of health-care decisions to individuals and their doctors, we will likely see more examples of this ghoulish approach to "patient care."

An Accelerated Physician Shortage

The Department of Health and Human Services promised that Obamacare would help "expand the number of primary-care doctors, nurses, and physician assistants." It's done the opposite. A 2015 study by the Association of American Medical Colleges projects a shortfall of over 90,000 physicians in the U.S. by 2025.

By vastly increasing the patient burden on doctors and making it harder than ever to make a living, Obamacare is driving many doctors to abandon their practices or seek early retirement. Commentator Charles Krauthammer, who has an M.D. in psychiatry, noted that classmates at his medical school's 40th reunion were totally demoralized: "The complaint was not financial but vocational—an incessant interference with their work, a deep erosion of their autonomy and authority, a transformation from physician to 'provider.'"

Krauthammer writes that a major Obamacare burden on physicians has been the law's requirement to computerize patient medical records. Doctors who don't comply are subject to penalties that cut their already paltry reimbursements. "Consider the myriad small practices that, facing ruinous transition costs in equipment, software, training and time, have closed shop, gone bankrupt or been swallowed by some larger entity."

The electronic health records (EHR) mandate is turning physicians into paper pushers. A study in the *American Journal of Emergency Medicine* found that doctors in the ER spend the bulk of their time—43%—entering electronic records information, 28% with patients.

Shrinking reimbursements from Medicare and Medicaid can mean some physicians who have trained for over a decade and have an education—and resulting debt—worth well into the six figures can get paid as little as $25 for a visit.

Doctors today now see nearly twice the number of patients they saw 40 years ago. Yet the average inflation-adjusted income of a general practitioner has fallen dramatically, from $185,000 in 1970 to just $161,000 in the last decade. Obamacare's cost pressures are also destroying once-lucrative private practices, forcing many doctors into large, impersonal groups based in hospitals. The result: care that is less personal and driven by government political priorities, not the patient's.

The Cato Institute's Michael Tanner laments, "Medicine is simply no longer the profession that it once was." Its diminished rewards have meant that American medical school graduates are discouraged from becoming primary care internists at a time when aging Baby Boomers are driving up demand. More foreign-trained doctors are treating Americans. But there are not even enough of them to fill the gap.

We would not have a doctor shortage if American healthcare were unencumbered by government cost controls. Just the way soaring demand for computers attracted the greatest entrepreneurial talent into high tech—Steve Jobs, Bill Gates, Jeff Bezos, and others—demand for medical treatment would produce a similar "gold rush" into medical care. If we are to continue attracting the best and the brightest into healthcare, we must remove governmental cost controls.

Higher-Cost Health Insurance and Medical Care

Every day, Obamacare's official moniker—The Patient Protection and *Affordable* Care Act—looks more Orwellian. In 2008, candidate Barack Obama promised that his administration's healthcare reform would save families $2,500 a year on health insurance premiums. If only that had been true. Since Obamacare was passed, insurance premiums have gone up and deductibles have risen sharply.

Remember the millions of Americans initially kicked off their health insurance when the Act went into effect in 2014? Most ended up with more expensive plans and inferior coverage. Typical was the experience of 56-year-old Arkansas mom Wanda Buckley. The replacement plan recommended by her insurance company was more expensive than her current $400-a-month plan and would cost as much as a whopping $22,000 a year. Worse still, it forced her family to pay for things like pediatric care and substance abuse treatment, services they would never use. She complained at the time, "The Obamacare plans just don't give us the coverage we want at a price we can afford—and Obamacare basically makes it illegal for us to tailor a health plan that does."

Since then the cost of insurance and care has continued to go up. In 2015, a study of healthcare benefits and spending by the actuarial firm Milliman reported that the annual cost of health-care for a typical American family of four—both employer-paid benefits and employee out-of-pocket costs—reached $24,671—up more than $5,200, or 27%, since 2011. Milliman predicts the num-ber to almost certainly surpass $25,000 in 2016.

Americans holding private insurance plans not purchased on Obamacare exchanges are seeing premiums skyrocket, and the increases keep coming. Grace-Marie Turner of the Galen Institute wrote in USA Today that in 2015, "Health insurers across the country are seeking premium increases of 20% to 40% or more." Furthermore, she warns, "Next year, businesses with 51 to 100 employees must comply with a battery of new ACA regulations estimated to increase premiums by an average of 18% for 150,000 businesses covering 7 million workers and dependents."

Why has this happened? Obamacare doubled down on the regulations that were previously driving up the cost of insurance— and then some. Insurers are unable to set their rates based on their actual costs. Writes healthcare analyst Sally Pipes, "Obamacare covers high-risk individuals in the most expensive way possible— by guaranteeing coverage for all comers, throwing all patients into the same pool, and prohibiting insurers from charging high-cost patients any more than three times what they charge the lowest-cost patients."

Under the law's age rating restrictions, an insurer can't charge a 64-year-old a rate that is more than three times what it charges a 21-year-old for the same plan. Yet 64-year-olds as a group are sicker and more expensive to cover. The law's benefit mandates requiring a level of coverage bureaucrats deemed "essential" hiked up costs even beyond state mandates. All of these mandates have helped drive up costs.

Before Obamacare, insurance premiums were rising because of state mandates forcing insurers to cover a host of things patients may not have necessarily needed or wanted. According to various estimates, such mandates raised the cost of coverage 30% to 50%.

Healthcare analysts such as Sally Pipes believe that Obamacare's perverse incentives will continue to drive up costs. The law's mandate forcing insurers to take all comers, she explains, "gives people a strong incentive to go without coverage until they get sick. As premiums rise to offset the costs of the folks using their coverage to pay for needed care, relatively healthy individuals will increasingly drop their policies. This process will repeat itself until insurance is unaffordable for everyone."

Obamacare is about redistribution. The privately insured are paying hefty premiums to subsidize individuals on low-income plans. The young subsidize the old. Young, healthy people have seen marked premium increases under Obamacare. Sean Parnell of the Heartland Institute writes, "Millennials in some states were hit with double-digit increases. In Alaska, young enrollees in Obamacare saw their premiums increase 28 percent [from $341.58 per month in 2014 to $437.22 in 2015]. This is comparable with the 28 percent increase among 50-year-old Alaskans and the 24 percent increase for family rates."

Obamacare supporters will reply that the law has slowed the overall rise of healthcare premiums, and that the cost of plans purchased over state healthcare exchanges hasn't risen all that much. To understand how misleading this is, all you need do is look at the deductibles. According to a study by the firm HealthPocket, the average deductible on a 2015 Bronze Obamacare plan is on average *almost more than four times higher* than deductibles on employer-offered plans. In other words, people with moderate or low incomes needing low-cost health insurance have to pay more out of pocket for healthcare than higher-income, privately insured patients.

Also helping drive up costs is consolidation in the healthcare sector. Anti-trust liberals ostensibly hate "monopolies." Yet the proliferation of regulations has created a health insurance market where only the largest players can afford to compete. A 2014 study by the American Medical Association found that more than 70% of metro areas have "highly concentrated" health insurance markets. In the vast majority of the nation's metropolitan areas, one health insurer dominated 30% or more of the market. In 45 states, the two largest health insurers have a lock on 50% or more of the market.

The same trend is underway with hospitals, both profit-based and nonprofit. Chains are gobbling up hospitals, clinics, and physician practices to give them negotiating leverage with both the government and insurers. Washington likes this: it's much easier to regulate a handful of entities than a diffuse and diverse marketplace.

A Drag on the Economy Created by the Employer Mandate and a Slew of New Taxes

By forcing companies with 50 or more full-time employees to offer health insurance, Obamacare's mandate (also known as "Obamatax") penalizes entrepreneurial job creators for growing and creating full-time jobs. You don't need to be an economist to guess the effect on the economy. CNNMoney.com reported in 2014:

> Overall U.S. unemployment has fallen steeply in the past year (from 7.2% in October 2013 to 5.8% in October 2014), but too many people *can only find part-time positions.* (Emphasis added) The number of people working part-time involuntarily is more than 50% higher than when the recession began.
>
> There was a similar spike in part-time workers in prior recessions, but it dropped quickly. That's not happening this time around. In fact, some states have seen an increase during the recovery in people languishing in part-time jobs who want something more.

Also weighing down the economy is Obamacare's estimated $569 billion in new and increased taxes and fees. They include: taxes on high-cost "Cadillac" health insurance plans; a hike in the Medicare payroll tax, from 2.9% to 3.8% for high-income earners; additional taxes on investment income; an increase in the threshold for deducting medical expenses, from 7.5% of adjusted gross income to 10%, for all taxpayers under the age of 65; increased taxes on brand name prescription drugs; a 2.3% sales tax on medical devices; additional taxes on insurance companies, based on an assessment of the insurer's market share. There's even a 5% tax on tanning salons. Each of these levies, in addition to Obamacare regulations, increases the burden on businesses and siphons wealth from the economy. All told, healthcare analyst Michael Tanner predicts,

> Accurately measured, the Patient Protection and Affordable Care Act will cost more than $2.7 trillion over its first 10 years of full operation, and add more than $823 billion to the national debt. And this does not even include more than $4.3 trillion in costs shifted to businesses, individuals, and state governments.

Declining Medical Innovation

Developers of medical innovations are being hit especially hard by Obamacare levies—especially those on medical devices and drugs. In 2014, Dr. Scott Atlas wrote in the *Wall Street Journal* that the law had already begun to make the U.S. less hospitable to medical research and development:

> According to *R&D Magazine* and the research firm Battelle, growth of R&D spending in the U.S. from 2012 to 2014 averaged just 2.1%, down from an average of 6% over the previous 15 years. In that same 15-year period, Malaysia, Thailand, Singapore, South Korea, India and the European Union saw faster R&D spending growth than the U.S. China's grew on average 22% per year.

Atlas acknowledges that some of this slowdown has to do with the post-2008 recession. And medical entrepreneurs have long had to contend with hellacious red tape placed in their path by bureaucrats at the Food and Drug Administration, which has made getting approval for new drugs and devices harder than in other developed countries. But he says it's the new Obamacare taxes that are now hammering medical innovators. Atlas writes,

The CEO of one of the largest health-care companies in America recently told me that the device tax his company paid last year exceeded his company's entire R&D budget. Already a long list of companies—including Boston Scientific, Stryker, and Cook Medical—have announced job cuts and plans to open new centers for R&D, manufacturing, and clinical trials overseas.

Along with rationing America's medical care in the here and now, Obamacare's taxes and regulations are preventing future life-saving treatments from being developed. If we are to save healthcare and revive America, this pernicious law must be stopped. The next chapter explains how.

CHAPTER 3

What to Do Now: Steve's Plan for Revolutionizing Healthcare

WITH ITS NUMEROUS ECONOMIC AND POLITICAL COMplexities, doubters insist that it's impossible to reform healthcare. They're wrong. Remove today's constraints, and you'll see big changes happen quickly. Think about how different our lives were little more than a decade ago, before the Internet grew into what it is today. There was no Netflix or Facebook. Amazon only sold books. Internet music was in its infancy. Online shopping was nowhere near the level it is now. A cell phone was just a phone and not a handheld computer. Allow innovation to occur in healthcare the way it does in consumer technology, and you'll soon see advances that are currently unimaginable.

Such breakthroughs promise to dramatically lower costs and improve the quality of care—if their widespread adoption is not impeded by Obamacare's massive regulations. One example is the field of genomics. DNA sequencing is giving rise to the new field of personalized medicine that is developing treatments based on a patient's genetic profile. To date, some 268,000 human genomes

37

have been sequenced, and the process is becoming faster and cheaper. A few years ago sequencing a human genome cost $10 million. Today it costs $1,000. Within a few years it will drop to $100.

Catherine Wood, a noted technology analyst and head of ARK Investment Management, says the sequencing explosion is already revolutionizing diagnostics. She cites the example of tests for thyroid cancer. Right now, when diagnosing that disease, "the results can be impossible to classify as malignant or benign." An estimated $500 million is spent annually on unnecessary thyroid surgery. A new genetically based test developed by Veracyte, a San Francisco-based biotech firm, offers a solution. The test "costs less than 25% of the lifetime cost of thyroid surgery and medication and informs doctors and patients with absolute surety whether or not they have thyroid cancer."

But, for these new technologies to truly revolutionize health-care, we need a dynamic, *patient-controlled* market that will encourage—indeed *demand*—such entrepreneurial advances. Patients are currently unable to benefit from many new treatments because third-party insurers deem them "too expensive" to cover. Almost no one, including many medical professionals, fully grasps how such costs have been artificially inflated by government con-straints across the system.

This would quickly change in an open market where patients— not government, large corporations, or hospitals—would make the critical buying decisions. If you, the patient, had control of the healthcare dollar, the market would be about meeting your needs, not those of your employer or insurance provider. A major objec-tive of reform must also be to eliminate the countless regulations restricting competition and choice that drive up costs.

Removing these strictures and permitting people to buy their own insurance and care would push insurers and caregivers to come up with new, less expensive ways of delivering services. Insurers, doctors, and hospitals seeking to attract and retain your business would become more accountable; they'd pay greater attention to customer service. You'd be treated with the kind of attention you get in stores and hotels.

What about the cost-inflation caused by Medicare and Medicaid, whose paltry reimbursements push healthcare providers to shift their costs to the privately insured? Even if we retain those programs, it would be easier for government to afford them because a consumer market would bring overall costs down.

This is illustrated by the relatively low cost of plastic surgery and laser vision surgery. Neither is normally covered by traditional health insurance unless the surgery is needed because of accident or disease. Plastic surgery has not experienced the kind of price inflation that has afflicted the rest of the healthcare industry, even though it has grown more than sixfold over the past 20 years and has experienced a number of technological breakthroughs. Conventional laser eye surgery that reshapes the cornea so a patient no longer needs to wear glasses, costs a third less in real terms than it did at the turn of the century.

Supporters of government healthcare say that consumer-driven care does not address the issue of pre-existing conditions. Actually it does. Insuring the poorest and sickest people is easier when care is cheaper. Lower prices also mean that a smaller segment of the population would be unable to afford healthcare and need assistance. A consumer-driven healthcare market, therefore, would make it easier to offer safety nets to people with pre-existing conditions through such programs as state high-risk pools with subsidized premiums.

What specific reforms are necessary to bring about a consumer-driven market—and liberate American healthcare? Here's our list.

Medicare Should Require That Healthcare Providers, Particularly Hospitals and Clinics, Post Prices for All Procedures and Services

Healthcare prices should be available to consumers the way prices are for just about every other product or service. That way, for example, patients can find the prices that various hospitals charge for an MRI and comparison shop. Right now there are only a handful of "price transparency" services like healthcarebluebook .com and castlighthealth.com. Since patients don't pay the bills, there's limited demand for them. In a real consumer market, this would quickly change. Online services would mushroom, just as they have in the travel industry and other sectors of the economy. Informed consumers make better decisions, leading to a more efficient market, with downward pressure on prices.

Create a National Market for Insurance and Larger Risk Pools by Allowing Consumers to Shop for Coverage Across State Lines

Even before Obamacare, health insurance premiums were inflated by state regulations and mandates that segmented the market into small, inefficient state risk pools. This has meant that insurers recoup their costs from a limited number of policyholders through higher premiums.

All of this would change if people could buy insurance across state lines. Allow individuals to purchase insurance from any company in any state. For example, if you don't like the expensive plans offered in New York State, you could buy cheaper coverage in a state that doesn't mandate coverage for things you may not need, like acupuncture or fertility treatments. This would create a more competitive national market. More players and plans would compete for your business. Premiums would start to drop. Policy offerings, and customer service, would improve.

Before the passage of Obamacare, a study by healthcare econ-omists at the University of Minnesota found that allowing people to purchase health insurance from out of state would enable more people to be covered. According to researchers, a national market would have reduced the number of uninsured by as many as 17 mil-lion; combined with tax reforms (see the next section), this policy would have covered as many as 24 million uninsured Americans.

The quickest route to a competitive national market for health insurance is for Congress to pass a law mandating it. But there is also another, less efficient way. States can enter into inter-state compacts that might permit them to nullify or opt out of the Affordable Care Act insurance regulations. Such interstate arrangements have been used in the past to settle boundary dis-putes and other issues.

Some are already offering "multi-state" insurance plans. As of 2014, such plans are offered in some 30 states.

Forbes opinion editor Avik Roy has pointed out that such alli-ances have the potential over time to create a national market: "Insurers would ultimately have an incentive to build these multi-state plans, because they would have larger risk pools, reducing the volatility of health-care spending, and reducing administrative costs." Interstate pacts would increase competition in the delivery of care: "In the many parts of the country where metropolitan areas border several states, insurers could build multi-state provider networks, increasing competition among hospitals and other providers."

Right now, multi-state plans are having a very limited impact thanks to the overriding constraints of Obamacare—for example, they have to offer the ACA's "essential benefits." And they can't do much to increase competition when there are only one or two other insurance providers in a market. But multi-state plans should become available in all states by 2017. That's a start. But you would see many more plans and benefits to consumers if Obamacare restrictions were removed.

Equal Tax Treatment: Both Individuals and Employers Should Get Tax Deductions for Buying Health Insurance (That Is, If There Isn't a Flat Tax Yet)

We mentioned in the previous chapter how the employer-based market for health insurance came about following the tax deduction given in 1954 to employers that offered health insurance to their workers. This tax advantage helped create the system of "third-party pay" responsible for much of what's ailing healthcare. Employer-based insurance can also hold people back, because it discourages them from leaving their jobs—and taking risks—when they fear losing their coverage.

Why should only businesses and the self-employed get tax deductions for buying insurance? Why shouldn't individuals? Why shouldn't you be able to pay for your healthcare in pre-tax dollars? Giving all individuals a deduction would encourage more people to purchase insurance and help to create a more broad-based market. After all, a person may feel that her company's plan is inadequate. Under the current system, it is extremely difficult to forgo that plan and buy your own.

Equal tax treatment would encourage Americans to buy their own insurance coverage, spurring the growth of the market for individuals. It would result in a much larger market for individual policies, instead of the one-size-fits-all corporate policies that dominate today. Insurers would be accountable to individual patients and would be compelled to deliver more reliable, affordable coverage.

Remove Obamacare's Costly Coverage Mandates

Obamacare's coverage mandates force insurers to provide a raft of benefits—whether or not the individual wants them. This top-down central planning has destroyed the original concept of insurance—

that it is supposed to cover catastrophic events. Dramatically worsened by Obamacare, coverage mandates have helped make health insurance prohibitively expensive, especially for young people.

They have also helped keep new entrants out of the insurance market. Even federally subsidized Consumer Operated and Oriented Plans [CO–OPs]—nonprofit cooperatives that are favorites of progressives—have been a failure. Many are struggling or have gone bust.

Removing coverage diktats could lower premium costs as much as 44% for younger adults and 7% for pre-retirement older adults, according to the Heritage Foundation. A 21-year-old would save $1,100 a year and a 64-year-old would save nearly $500. Freeing up the market would make it easier for new types of policies and consumer choices to emerge.

Encourage the Growth of Tax-Free Health Savings Accounts

Health savings accounts (HSAs) are IRA-like accounts that enable you to set aside tax-free dollars to pay for healthcare. Under current law, you and/or your employer are permitted to contribute a defined amount of money to the account each year, just as you would to your IRA. In 2015, most people were allowed to contribute up to $3,350 for individuals and up to $6,650 for families. The money in the account is used to pay for routine medical expenses. What you don't spend remains in the account, earning tax-free interest, and rolls over into the following year. And, as with IRAs, you're allowed to invest the money in stocks, mutual funds, bonds, and CDs through a financial institution that acts as a trustee.

To open a health savings account, you have to have insurance with a deductible of at least $1,300 for individuals and $2,600 for family coverage. The health savings account is a more attractive option for employees than the flexible spending account generally used for dental and vision expenses, where the worker can lose money that hasn't been spent by year's end. It encourages people to use insurance for what it is supposed to be for—catastrophic expenses. In this way, HSAs help bring down the cost of premiums. They also promote a consumer-driven market by encouraging the patient to pay directly for routine medical care.

Caps limiting HSA contributions should be removed or substantially raised. If people wish to put more money aside for medical expenses, why not?

Another flaw of HSAs today is that funds can only be used for expenses incurred after you opened the account. Talk about hurting people with pre-existing conditions! And if you use the money for non-medical expenses, you will find yourself liable for federal income tax and a 20% penalty.

For years, Forbes Media has provided employees with health savings accounts. The company gives each employee $2,500 a year, which covers most or all of the deductible. Money that isn't used is rolled over. If medical bills exceed both that $2,500 and the employee portion of the deductible, traditional health insurance kicks in. When companies initially put such a plan in place, they often see a decline in premiums. Over time, Forbes' premiums have increased less than those of its peers. Because the deductible is high, the insurance is a relative bargain.

The irony of the Affordable Care Act is that the high deductibles of plans on Obamacare exchanges have caused HSAs, with their tax advantages, to become more attractive. According to a 2014 industry report, the number of HSAs and health reimbursement arrangements increased some 150% from 2008. Total account balances came to more than $22 billion, compared with just $7.7 billion in 2010. The proportion of people covered by employer plans using these types of accounts has jumped from 3% in 2006 to 23% in 2014.

HSAs would probably grow even faster if, as we suggest above, government would remove current restrictions on qualifying deductibles and how much money you can put in your account.

Obamacare rules also make HSAs less attractive to families. That's because 24- to 26-year-old young adults on family policies don't have access to the accounts. If such restrictions were loosened, you would see faster growth in the marketplace. Another phenomenon would unfold: growing amounts of money would accumulate in these accounts. Thanks to the miracle of compounding interest, they would become a significant asset that people could rely on to finance their care.

Those flexible spending accounts for dental and eye care that we mentioned above should also be reformed. Current law allows employees to contribute up to $2,500 a year tax free to pay for certain medical expenses. The rules mandate that almost all the money in FSAs be spent each year and only $500 can be carried over into the following year. This restriction should be removed. This would enable people to set more money aside for dental and eye care expenses.

Why Not HSAs for Medicare?

Medicare beneficiaries should have the option to use HSAs. The best way to bring about change is to give people a choice. Beneficiaries, if they desired, could stay with the current system. Those who wish to use the HSA provision would receive, say, $10,000 a year for regular expenses. Any money they did not use would, as in the regular HSA, roll over. They would have true catastrophic insurance if an individual's annual expense ran above that $10,000. As we know, catastrophic insurance, even for the elderly, is relatively cheap with a high deductible. In other words, the government would save money even though it would cover the deductible. Patients/beneficiaries in charge of their money would exert downward pressure on costs. Today, under the present system, if a doctor recommends a battery of tests, a Medicare patient does not have the incentive to ask, "why?" A Medicare

HSA would change that. The passive patient would become a consumer tiger.

Medicare Should Require That Hospitals Post Each Month How Many Patients Have Died from Hospital-Based Infections

A patient going for a knee replacement shouldn't end up dying from sepsis. Posting hospital infection rates will not only lead to better patient care, it will also help eliminate the substantial costs associated with treating those same secondary infections picked up in the hospital.

Medicare Should Require That Healthcare Providers Post Each Year How Much They Received in Medicare Payments

This would quickly curb abuses. There was a U.S. District Court decision in 1979 that held that Medicare couldn't reveal the earnings of individual doctors under the program. While this prohibition has been chipped away, Congress should override this by legislating such a mandate. Medicare fraud has been estimated to be as high as $90 billion annually.

Current Federal Spending on Medicaid Should Be Given to the States as Grants

Let the states running Medicaid decide how best to use this money. This way we can see what works. Best practices would quickly be transferred from state to state, increasing the overall efficiency of the market, again lowering overall costs. The likely result would be that most states would give beneficiaries the equivalent of medical savings accounts, and they can shop for the best offerings.

Of Course, Obamacare Should Be Repealed

If it isn't, the following provisions should be jettisoned: the employer mandate, the individual mandate, and the cap on insurance company profit margins.

That cap is especially pernicious. Under Obamacare, insurers must spend 80%–85% of premiums on reimbursements. This plays to liberal fantasies that insurers spend too much on executive compensation, advertising, other administrative expenses, dividends, and stock buybacks. The rule has two perverse consequences—it incentivizes insurers to expand revenues, which means insurers have no incentive to control healthcare costs. The more costs, the more revenue—and the more profit. This rule is a barrier to insurance start-ups that by definition begin with higher expenses until they achieve meaningful size. In other words, it blocks competition.

We should also relegate to the dustbin of recent history the Independent Payment Advisory Board, the Obamacare bureaucracy supposed to make "tough choices" cutting Medicare spending. In the real world this translates into restricting care for the elderly. And, finally, eliminate the electronic health records mandate. This has led to systems that don't meet the particular needs of the individual medical specialties, hospitals, and clinics. In free markets, there are infinite varieties of systems that customers and businesses find useful. One size fits all is a disaster and a huge waste of money.

PART TWO

ENACT A FLAT TAX:
Revive America by Slaying the Tax Beast

CHAPTER 4

Why We Need Radical Tax Reform *Now*

THE SECOND OF OUR BIG THREE REFORMS TARGETS THE federal income tax code. Year after year, this toxic leviathan tightens its grip around the American people. How did that happen in America, a nation founded on tax protests and the rallying cry of the American Revolution—"No taxation without representation"? Back then, the way the British decided to tax tea so enraged Bostonians that they swarmed British ships, tossing crates of the stuff into Boston Harbor. And that historic melee, the Boston Tea Party, was ignited by a *single* tax. What would the colonists think of America in the 21st century, when just about everything is subject to some kind of tax?

Consider a typical day. Get up in the morning and turn on the lights, and you're paying taxes and fees on your electricity. Then turn on the water. More fees and taxes on your water bill. Enjoy your morning cup of coffee or tea—and you've paid sales taxes. Walk the dog? It's almost time to renew Fido's license. Then off to work—you're paying gasoline taxes and perhaps a toll or two.

Start your workday at the office and you're racking up federal income taxes, state income taxes, Social Security taxes, and Medicare taxes. On the way home after work, maybe you go shopping. Not only do you get hit with sales taxes, you also pay the

51

hidden costs of levies the stores themselves pay and are quietly passing on to you, the customer.

But this taxing day is not over: you get home and a notice in your mailbox announces that your property taxes are going up. Want to complain? That email you're about to send is being transmitted by a computer or mobile device that rings up still more taxes. Even the Internet itself is no longer a tax-free zone. There is a quiet move afoot in Congress to impose sales taxes on all Internet transactions.

And we haven't even gotten to the federal income tax code—the biggest abomination of all. Abraham Lincoln's Gettysburg Address, which defined the character of the American nation, was all of 272 words. The Declaration of Independence, about 1,300 words. The Constitution with all of its amendments, about 8,000 words. The Holy Bible, which took centuries to put together, 773,000 words. The federal income tax code and all its attendant rulings and interpretations has been estimated to be about 10 million words and rising.

This is because the rules even have rules. Alongside of the federal tax code is something called the "Federal Tax Regulations" that's supposed to amplify what's in the code. It runs several times the length of the code itself and is all too often incomprehensible. Then there are hundreds of IRS tax forms and several hundred other forms to explain how to fill out those forms. And on and on it goes. Taxpayers are deluged.

Even Barack Obama has called for simplifying this mess. The current system is a bureaucratic monstrosity that is dragging down our economy and preventing Americans from all walks of life from getting ahead. But the burden of the code goes beyond the financial. It is undermining our values, social trust, and quality of life as a society. But to fully appreciate the need for reform, you have to know just how bad the situation is.

Complexity and Confusion

The code is so complex that, unlike Obamacare, you can read it and *still* not know what's in it. Several years ago, *Money* magazine took a hypothetical family's finances and gave the numbers to 46 tax preparers who were asked to prepare the family's tax returns. What came back? The magazine received 46 returns with 46 different estimates—in some cases running into the thousands of dollars—of what the family owed. This from experts considered the best in the business.

Thanks to the code's Byzantine system of regulations and formulas, taxes that individuals and businesses pay can vary wildly. What you end up owing the government can depend on the tax software you happen to use.

Take the hypothetical example of "Richard," a single man whose $50,000 in earnings and expenses were entered into several tax software programs on the market. TurboTax said the government owed him a $235 refund. FreeTaxUSA said he owed $244. TaxACT said he owed $775. And, finally, H&R Block said he owed the government $997.

Which one was right? The programs were all designed by tax experts. And yet there was a $1,232 difference between the lowest and the highest estimates of Richard's tax liability.

No one truly understands what's in the code, not even the IRS. The agency's hot line has long been known for giving taxpayers wrong answers—though they give far fewer today because the beleaguered agency has scaled back customer service and now answers only "basic" questions.

Americans pay for all of the confusion with needless tax penalties and emotional distress. Taxpayer Paul Hatz was a victim of this kind of IRS ignorance. Through the error of an IRS auditor, Hatz was hit with a $110,000 personal tax bill for a liability that wasn't his. The audit process forced him to close his small business, which employed about a dozen people in his community, and cost him the $100,000 investment he had made in his company as well.

"This 'tax' was all because the auditor miscategorized money I invested into [my company] as 'income,'" Hatz told *DailyFinance*. "I never want to start a business again. Large corporations with teams of tax attorneys and CPAs can deal with an audit. If you get the wrong auditor and are a small business struggling to make ends meet, you are done—out of business regardless of whether you did anything wrong or not."

When government contractor Glen Wiggy went to Iraq in 2008, both he and his employer thought a provision in the code meant that the income he earned there would be exempt from federal taxes. Then he learned that the exemption applied to just a single tax year from January to December. Because Wiggy was in Iraq between June 2008 and June 2009, he didn't qualify, and ended up having to pay nearly $30,000.

These are just two of the countless law-abiding taxpayers penalized as a result of the code's mind-numbing complexity. Whether it's middle-class families forced to pay the Alternative Minimum Tax that targets the wealthy, or a simple misunderstanding of complex deductions that results in a penalty of thousands of dollars, the tax system all too often subjects Americans to a painful assault that is not just anxiety-producing—it's unfair.

Unfair!

Little wonder that no one today thinks the system is just. The "99%" think the "1%" don't pay enough. The 1% are steamed by the idea that almost 50% of people don't pay any income taxes.

Both sides are wrong. Contrary to what the left frequently claims, the top 1% of income earners pay *more* than their fair share. They accounted for nearly half of Uncle Sam's income tax receipts in 2014, according to a study by the non-partisan Tax

Policy Center. The top 20% shouldered more than 80% of the burden, while the bottom 50% paid less than 3%.

Nor is it true—as those in higher brackets maintain—that people in the lowest brackets don't pay taxes. Every worker pays taxes for Social Security and Medicare, though Uncle Sam insists these levies are not really taxes but rather mandatory contributions for retirement income and health benefits.

The truth is that *everyone* pays taxes. But seemingly arbitrary, confusing, and varying rates create the appearance of unfairness. Another example: the widespread misunderstanding of capital gains taxes. Warren Buffett famously complained that the system is unfair because his tax rate is lower than his secretary's. But capital gains taxes are lower for a reason. The lower rates are in recognition of the fact that gains are reaped from money invested and put *at risk* to the benefit of the economy. Warren Buffett, or an average stockholder, may have realized gains. But he, or any investor, could have just as easily lost that money. Such investment and risk taking are what creates jobs and growth in our economy, which is why capital gains taxes are traditionally lower.

Nonetheless, the lower rate, like so much in the tax code, encourages social resentment. Like acid, the code over time corrodes our belief in the fairness of our economic and political systems.

Corruption and Cronyism

What *is* unfair about the code is how it has polluted the political process. The system is stacked in favor of individuals and corporations that can afford tax lawyers to navigate the code's confusing regulations—or hire lobbyists to win tax breaks from government.

There was a time when corporations primarily lobbied Washington to keep government *out* of their business. That has changed. In the words of *The Atlantic*, "[T]he evolution of business lobbying from a sparse reactive force into a ubiquitous and increasingly proactive one is among the most important transformations in American politics over the last 40 years."

This favor-seeking is usually centered on getting special treatment and tax breaks. The total cost of lobbying Congress is now greater than the cost of *running* Congress. Roughly $2.6 billion is spent each year on lobbying, while less than $2 billion is needed to run the national legislature.

Tax loopholes can produce market distortions and destructive, unintended consequences. Remember, our third-party payer system in healthcare—and its toxic distortions that helped give us Obamacare—began with a tax break for corporations seeking to provide health insurance to their employees.

Washington politicians also use the code to advance their political agendas by rewarding breaks—or in Washington-speak, "incentives"—to politically favored projects or special interests. The Obama administration has handed out tax breaks for investment in alternative energy technologies—for example, biomass and biofuel. In addition to being a waste of our money, these incentives help prop up expensive technologies that would otherwise fail in the market.

Compliance—A Hidden Tax

The taxes themselves are only part of the cost of this toxic code. There's also the cost of compliance that is a second hidden tax. Think about all that you have to go through, as an individual or business owner, pulling together records, hiring and paying an accountant, reviewing your returns. Then there's the time and energy spent on dealing with the government during an audit. A study from the Mercatus Center at George Mason University puts the annual cost of compliance as high as $378 billion and the total annual economic cost (including work hours) at more than $600 billion.

Compliance doesn't just cost money. It diverts resources that could be better used elsewhere in the economy. Imagine all those bright minds and $600 billion reinvested every year into something that was actually productive. The resulting boom in the economic, technological, and academic arenas would be immediate and amazing.

Taxes Are "a Cost and a Burden"— and a Drag on the Economy

What politicians—not only in the U.S. but around the world—don't understand is that taxes punish work and productivity. How do nanny-state pols seek to discourage things like smoking and sugary drinks? They tax them. Politicians create similar disincentives when they raise taxes on productive individuals and businesses.

Taxes are a cost and a burden on people and productivity. Your income tax is the price you pay for working. The tax on profit that your business makes is the price you pay for being successful. The tax you pay on capital gains is the price you pay for taking risks that pan out.

Lower the price of productive work, risk taking and success, and you'll get more of those good things, spurring economic growth and job creation. After tax cuts proposed by Democratic President John F. Kennedy were enacted in the mid-1960s, the economy soared. From 1961 to 1968, federal revenue increased by 62%.

Nearly two decades later, in 1981, President Ronald Reagan instituted an across-the-board income tax cut that lowered rates by 23%—the top rate of 70% was reduced to 50%. Another round of cuts in 1986 reduced the top income tax rate from 50% to 28%. Despite the protests of naysayers who projected a massive drop in government revenue, federal revenue soared during the Reagan era and the national net wealth increased by $17 trillion, 10 times the increase in the national debt. Reagan's tax cuts freed the economy of its Carter-era lethargy. After killing inflation in 1982, the U.S. experienced over 4% annual growth in our GDP and a net increase of 16.1 million new jobs between 1983 and 1989.

On the other hand, when taxes are raised too high, they discourage work and productivity. According to one analysis, a 1% hike in the personal income tax rate translates into a reduction in real GDP per capita of up to approximately 3%.

Our tax code is one reason why our economy has yet to return to the growth rates of the 1980s and 1990s. America's corporate tax rate—which is almost 40% if you include state taxes—is the highest among the world's major economies. According to the Tax Foundation, "If [the corporate tax rate] came down 10 points— still higher than most of our trading partners—it would add 1 to 2 points to GDP growth and likely not lose tax revenue."

The Code Gives the IRS Too Much Power

When any government agency becomes too large, the temptation is great for bureaucrats to abuse their power at the expense of our liberty. That is what's happening today. The gargantuan federal code requires more than 80,000 agents for collection and enforcement, enough people to populate a small city. No surprise that this giant agency has taken to abusing its power. The Obama administration's politicized IRS has harassed not only the Tea Party nonprofits but also pro-Israel groups and publications, delaying requests for nonprofit status and making draconian demands for information, including donor lists.

Another example of its power gone wrong is the IRS's civil asset seizure program, which has turned into a virtual criminal enterprise that confiscates the money of innocent Americans. The IRS can seize your bank account on the basis of simple suspicion that you've done something wrong. Even if you're found to have committed no wrongdoing, the IRS will try to keep your funds anyway. In 2014, the agency grabbed nearly $154,000 from the bank accounts of Khalid Quran, a Greenville, North Carolina convenience store owner, because his deposits fit a "suspicious" model under the Civil Asset Forfeiture Reform Act. Using this law, which was intended to fight mob crimes, the IRS targets taxpayers with a pattern of cash deposits and withdrawals known as "structuring." Despite the fact that he had committed no actual crime, the IRS pressured Mr. Quran, whose first language was Arabic, into signing a "Consent to Forfeiture" form.

Maryland dairy farmer Randy Sowers had more than $62,000 seized by the IRS because of the pattern of his deposits. Mr. Sowers earned all of his money through legal endeavors, yet the IRS saw fit to empty his bank account simply because he made large deposits on a regular schedule.

According to the Institute for Justice, the IRS engaged in some 600 forfeitures before public outcry forced the agency to pull back and basically discontinue the practice. As for the targeting of conservatives, the monster bureaucracy shows no such contrition. The IRS retains way too much power, with too many opportunities for abuse.

End the Fear and Loathing

All of these examples show why taxes are among our top three areas in need of reform. We must drive a stake through the heart of today's leviathan tax monster and replace the current system with a new one based on a single Flat Tax.

No more fear and loathing as April 15 approaches. No more worrying about whether you have your required records. No more confusion and complexity. You can literally fill out your fax form on a single page or with a few keystrokes on your computer.

This very simple change wouldn't just increase convenience. It would transform government, our economy, and our society by jettisoning the complexity that gives bureaucrats so much power. A Flat Tax will help us begin to scale back today's overreaching Big Government, with its favor-dispensers and special interests.

A single rate for all would eliminate the uncertainty and loopholes that cause so much anxiety and political divisiveness. Everyone would pay less—not only in taxes but also in compliance. Investment and job creation would skyrocket. We'd finally see a real recovery that would grow the tax base and—irony of ironies—ultimately generate more revenue for government. The Flat Tax would unleash our full national potential.

The last thing we need is another half-baked, Band-Aid solution. It's not enough to simply cut tax rates and reduce the number of tax brackets. Think of what happened in 1986 after the code was somewhat simplified: numerous tax shelters were eliminated and the number of brackets was reduced to two, 28% and 15%. But no sooner was the ink dry on that legislation than Washington politicians picked up their old habits. There have been more than 15,000 changes to the code, as Congress, at the behest of a swarm of locust-like lobbyists, snuck in clauses and amendments to favor particular individuals, companies, industries, nonprofits, and causes. Changes have been inserted in the code by well-placed senators or representatives that didn't come to light until months later.

If we're to have a full American revival, a Flat Tax is essential. And that's the flat-out truth.

CHAPTER 5

What Is a Flat Tax?

A FLAT TAX IS THE ONLY WAY TO DRIVE A STAKE THROUGH the heart of the IRS Beast once and for all. It will replace today's federal income tax code, the single biggest portion of the tax burden for half the population and the most abusive part of our tax system. Before we get too far along, we should mention that the Flat Tax does not replace Medicare and Social Security taxes, or, obviously, state and local taxes. Those are reforms for another day.

Under a Flat Tax, you would file your return filling out a single sheet of paper or postcard or by spending a few minutes on your computer. No more of the confusion and anxiety that come with today's process of preparing and filing your taxes. This simple reform will liberate us, as individuals and as a society, from the tax tyranny that has plagued Americans for decades.

For those harboring doubts, our Flat Tax reform would allow tax filers to choose between a Flat Tax and the old system. Such a choice would take away any anxieties about losing particular deductions. People could compare plans and judge for themselves. Once they do, just about everyone would opt for the simplicity of the Flat Tax. Once you check out the specifics of the plan and its benefits, the choice of a Flat Tax is a no-brainer.

Just One Single Rate: A 17% Tax on Incomes for Individuals and Corporations

Income is taxed once and only once. No more double or triple taxation. The single rate is absolutely critical. Whenever we put two or more tax rates together, they're like rabbits. They breed. We saw that with the 1986 reforms, which consisted of two rates. They've since multiplied into the seven we have today and, effectively, even more: as their incomes go up, people start to lose personal deductions, which means their actual marginal rates go up as well.

Generous Exemptions for Adults and Children

Contrary to what some people believe, a Flat Tax is actually progressive. There are personal exemptions, and they're far more generous than what we have now:

- Adults and children would get a $13,200 standard exemption. Single people who make less than that—i.e., part-timers—would pay no taxes.
- Married couples would receive a $26,400 deduction ($13,200 × 2).
- A family of four would pay no taxes on their first $52,800 in income. *Roughly half of all Americans would owe no taxes at all.* This $52,800 threshold, by the way, is more than double the current federal poverty level. The Flat Tax will thereby increase social and economic mobility and make substantial inroads in the fight against poverty.

Temporarily Retain the Earned Income Tax Credit (EITC)

The EITC effectively refunds Social Security and Medicare taxes for low-income families and can amount to an additional subsidy of more than $6,200. It's a complex relic of our current tax code; it should be changed later as part of entitlement reform. This Flat Tax would phase it out over five years.

More Generous Deductions

Compare the Flat Tax exemptions listed above to the code's 2015 deductions: Taxpayers start out with a $4,000 personal exemption. Single individuals are permitted to take an additional standard deduction of $6,300 dollars, for a total of $10,300 in personal exemptions. A married couple filing jointly now takes a standard deduction of $12,600, in addition to their two $4,000 personal exemptions, for a total of $20,600.

A Tax Cut for Every Taxpayer

The Flat Tax constitutes a tax break for every single taxpayer. Everyone would pay less than they do now, and in many cases those in the lowest income brackets would actually have a *negative* tax rate.

What Would Be Your Effective Tax Rate Under the Flat Tax?	
Annual Income	Effective Tax Rate (%)
All returns	9.1%
$1 to $5,000	−4.7
$5,000 to $10,000	−8.4
$10,000 to $15,000	−9.4
$15,000 to $20,000	−7.5
$20,000 to $25,000	−4.4
$25,000 to $30,000	−2.3
$30,000 to $40,000	2.5
$40,000 to $50,000	6.2

(continued on next page)

$50,000 to $75,000	8.4
$75,000 to $100,000	9.9
$100,000 to $200,000	11.5
$200,000 to $500,000	13.0
$500,000 to $1,000,000	13.6
$1,000,000 to $1,500,000	13.8
$1,500,000 to $2,000,000	13.4
$2,000,000 to $5,000,000	13.3
$5,000,000 to $10,000,000	13.3
$10,000,000 or more	12.7

An Additional Compliance "Tax Cut"

And then there's also the indirect tax cut resulting from the enormous reduction in compliance costs. No more anguished hours stressing over whether TurboTax or your accountant did a proper job. Shrinking your return to the size of a postcard, the Flat Tax would reduce the need for the armies of accountants and IRS bureaucrats that are part of the taxation industry.

How easy would it be to calculate your taxes under the Flat Tax? See below for yourself.

The Steve Forbes Flat Tax Form	
1. Wages and salary	
2. Number of family members	
3. Deductions for family members (multiply line 2 by $13,200)	
4. Taxable income (line 1 minus line 3)	
5. Pre-credit income tax (multiply line 4 by 17%)	
6. Earned income tax credit (see EITC rules)	
7. Total tax (line 5 minus 6)	

If the Flat Tax "only" managed to reduce our compliance costs by a mere 50%, Americans would collectively realize savings of more than $150 to $300 billion. That's a $150 billion injection into the economy. The effects of this would be instantaneous. According to John Dunham & Associates, a highly regarded economic research firm, implementing a Flat Tax would restore GDP growth to well over 4% for several years—the kind of growth that invigorated the country in the 1980s and 90s. Over the next decade, the national economy would be 25.9%—or $5.7 trillion—larger in real terms than what the Congressional Budget Office now forecasts.

No More Double Taxation

With the Flat Tax, income is taxed at the federal level once and only once, eliminating double taxation through levies like the capital gains tax and the Death Tax. A Flat Tax means that families that lose a loved one will be relieved of the additional pain of paying estate taxes and worrying about IRS audits.

Getting rid of double taxation is also good for retirees, because dividend income would no longer be taxable. Dividends have already been taxed at the corporate level. Social Security payments, annuities, and other retirement vehicles funded with after-tax dollars would not be subject to federal taxes. You already paid income tax on your Social Security tax throughout your working life.

Jettisoning taxes on dividends and capital gains will be a boon to the larger economy because it will spur saving and investment. Remember what we said in Chapter 4 about taxes being a price? As anyone knows who owns a stock, capital gains taxes are a major reason why people hold on to their stocks. So they buy or invest less. The Flat Tax would change all that. Doing away with the taxation on capital gains and dividends would stimulate economic activity by lowering the price of investing and capital creation. The result: we'll get more investment in growth- and job-creating ventures.

Corporations Get a Flat Tax, Too

The Flat Tax is the same for companies as individuals: a consistent, across the board, 17% tax on company profits, defined as the company's gross income after accounting for wages and salaries, purchases of goods and services necessary to the function and operation of the business, and purchases of assets like plants, buildings, and equipment.

Companies Could Expense All Investments— No More Depreciation Insanity

The Flat Tax would demolish the cluttered and confusing calculations regarding asset depreciation. Companies could expense all investments. Depreciation schedules and credits would go into the shredder. No more writing off the cost of the asset over a period of years. No more time spent trying to figure out if it qualifies for federal credit or accelerated depreciation. Businesses would be allowed to expense the purchase of long-term physical assets immediately.

There's more good news: businesses would be able to carry losses due to capital investments forward into future years. A construction company needing expensive heavy machinery—whose purchase results in a loss on that year's income statement—can carry the loss forward into subsequent years to reduce its tax liability until it's used up. This would allow entrepreneurs to invest more easily in their businesses. Companies will make investment decisions based on what makes good business sense instead of on tax implications.

The Flat Tax Would Increase Transparency and Close Corporate Loopholes

No more tax giveaways or advantageous tax exemptions for companies with deep pockets and powerful lobbyists. With the Flat

Tax, such loopholes would be closed. You'd see a massive decline in the influence of special interests and self-interested corporations.

The Flat Tax would also do away with the deduction of interest payments by businesses. This has long incentivized companies to risk loading up on debt. Interest on debt contracted before the Flat Tax would still be deductible.

The Flat Tax Will Only Tax Companies on the Income They Make in the United States

Today, American companies doing business abroad operate at a disadvantage. They compete against companies from such countries as France and the Netherlands that are only taxed within their own borders. Multinational American companies, in contrast, are subject not only to the taxes of countries in which they operate, but also U.S. taxes if they repatriate profits. They do get a credit for corporate taxes paid overseas, but the burden is still stiff because the U.S. has just about the highest profit tax in the world.

The United States' putative corporate taxes have encouraged the emergence of "transfer pricing"—a practice whereby multinationals shift costs to foreign divisions in order to be able to claim that products were produced overseas and thus avoid U.S. taxes. General Electric incurred political wrath in 2011 when it reported global profits of $14.2 billion, claiming that only $5.1 billion of those profits were generated in the United States.

Because it would be so much lower than the tax rates of most other nations, the corporate Flat Tax would encourage American companies to repatriate the trillions of dollars in profits they have artificially shifted overseas as a consequence of today's sky-high corporate tax rates.

With its low rate, the Flat Tax would also attract a flood of foreign capital into the U.S.

The Flat Tax Would Allow Companies to Increase Shareholder Dividends

In addition to being good for investors, the elimination of dividend levies under a Flat Tax encourages companies to increase dividends that benefit shareholders. That happened, for example, when the dividend tax was cut from 38% to 15% in 2003. Hundreds of companies raised their dividends, and dozens of companies that previously did not issue dividends began paying them, to the delight of their shareholders. In fact, Microsoft paid out around $30 billion in a special dividend in 2004 as a direct result of that decrease in the dividend tax.

The Flat Tax Would Not Do Away with Health Savings Accounts and IRAs

If you're one of the millions of Americans who owns a tax-free savings vehicle like an IRA or a health savings account, you may be wondering what happens to them under the Flat Tax. For existing accounts, the answer is: nothing. The money, after all, is yours. The good news is that the tax you pay on IRA distributions will likely drop dramatically.

There will still be a need for IRAs and HSAs in the future. You'll still need to save for retirement and healthcare. However, because there are no deductions under the Flat Tax—except for the personal exemptions—these vehicles will likely resemble what today is a Roth IRA. You'll put in after-tax dollars and the payout will be tax free. The same would be true of HSAs.

The Numbers Speak for Themselves: A Flat Tax Will Make the Economy Take Off Like a Rocket

The Obama administration's efforts to resuscitate the economy—including its notorious spending of hundreds of billions of dollars for "stimulus"—have been a stark failure. Median incomes are lower than they were in 2007—and far lower than at their peak in 1999. That's because the economy, weighed down by countless regulations and tax increases, is like a marathon runner forced to race in lead boots. President Obama signed into law a number of tax increases, including a top marginal tax rate of 39.6% and economy-killing hikes in capital gains taxes from 15 to nearly 24% (the rate includes a 3.8% investment tax levied under Obamacare). Then there's Obamacare itself, whose individual mandate has been deemed a "tax" by the Supreme Court. Obamacare has imposed a tax burden on entrepreneurial businesses forced to provide employees with health insurance or else face a penalty. It also has countless taxes and fees, such as the tax on medical devices, which are a further drag on the economy.

Just what would happen to the economy, and to your personal wealth, if a 17% Flat Tax were enacted tomorrow? We asked John Dunham & Associates to run the numbers. The results are astonishing. The chart below shows the U.S. growth rate as projected by the Congressional Budget Office over the next 10 years, compared with what it would be under the Flat Tax.

Comparison of Projected Economic Growth Under Flat Tax Versus Current Tax Code										
	2016	2017	2018	2019	2020	2021	2022	2023	2024	2025
Current Tax Code Growth Forecast (%) Congressional Budget Office	2.12	2.63	2.22	2.01	2.06	2.04	1.99	1.95	19.2	1.90
Flat Tax Growth Forecast (%)	7.48	6.36	4.84	4.20	4.05	3.90	3.72	3.65	3.07	2.98

You'd see similar acceleration in personal income. The next chart shows that it would increase at a greatly accelerated rate.

Comparison of Income Growth Projections Under Flat Tax Versus Current Tax Code		
Year	Current Tax Code (%)	Flat Tax (%)
2016	2.66	6.21
2017	2.74	5.34
2018	2.60	4.77
2019	2.38	4.14
2020	2.36	4.00
2021	2.45	3.85
2022	2.37	3.66
2023	2.31	3.60
2024	2.20	3.51
2025	2.09	3.42

The Flat Tax would put an end to the Obama era's declining wages. We'd see wage growth of historic proportions. The U.S. would once more return to its status as an economic powerhouse. What are we waiting for?

CHAPTER 6

Thriving Under
the Flat Tax

I N 2017, THE OBAMA YEARS OF STAGNATION AND TURMOIL will come to an end. A new president will take office. Americans eager to break from the past will be receptive to new solutions. The opportunity has never been greater to win political support to pass the Flat Tax. If we succeed, the United States would join more than 40 nations and jurisdictions that have adopted this system to revive stagnant or contracting economies. Among these are Russia, Romania, Lithuania, Hong Kong, Ukraine, and Hungary.

Why have so many other nations embraced a reform that people in the United States consider "radical"? Because their leaders recognize that succeeding in the global marketplace requires a pro-growth tax system that encourages a vigorous, entrepreneurial economy—and that the best way to achieve this is through a Flat Tax.

If only our leaders had such vision. The U.S. can't remain the world's foremost economic and political power unless something is done about today's toxic tax behemoth. To appreciate the potential of the Flat Tax to revive America, one need only look to the experiences of a few Flat Tax economies.

Hong Kong: The Granddaddy
of All Flat Tax Economies

The first to enact a Flat Tax in 1947, Hong Kong is the revolutionary pioneer of all Flat Tax economies. A former British colony, it was turned over to China as a special administrative region in 1997. Hong Kong's Flat Tax system has managed to weather decades of economic and political turbulence, including tensions with mainland China.

Hong Kong offers residents a choice: They can pay taxes under a traditional system of four graduated tax rates, ranging from 2% to 17%. These include deductions for charitable contributions and interest payments on home loans, as well as allowances for children, married couples, and dependents.

Or they can opt to pay the "Standard Rate," a 15% Flat Tax, if they fall into a higher bracket. The standard rate is paid by a tiny percentage of high-income residents. But it accounts for a substantially larger percentage of total tax revenue.

Because the standard rate is usually paid by taxpayers with incomes above a certain threshold, it has been compared to America's dreaded Alternative Minimum Tax. The comparison is absurd. Unlike the U.S., Hong Kong offers a *choice* between the two systems. In the United States, you're forced to pay whatever calculation is higher.

Hong Kong has another advantage over the U.S.: a corporate tax rate of 16.5%, and an even lower rate of 15% for small businesses. Hong Kong's tax system—and its business-friendly regulatory environment—has made the tiny region one of the world's centers of commerce. Only 427 square miles in size and with slightly more than 7 million residents, it has the ninth highest GDP per capita, according to the International Monetary Fund. Remarkably, it has suffered only one year of negative economic growth since the turn of the century.

A magnet for foreign investment, Hong Kong recently surpassed the United States and is now second in the world behind China, bringing in more than $100 billion in 2014. This pro-market tax system—and not Keynesian spending and devaluations—is the model China should adopt if it wants to again achieve rapid and sustainable growth.

Russia: A Formerly Communist Nation Becomes a Home for Billionaires

Before it enacted a Flat Tax in 2001, Russia's tax system was even more chaotic than ours. Conceived after the collapse of the Soviet Union, its federal code consisted of layers of levies. This mess was exacerbated by a tangle of local and regional taxes. Together they produced a corrupt and capricious regulatory environment that even Russians recognized was corrosive to their economy.

By the late 1990s, years of anti-growth, pro-inflation policies—including an inexplicable tax increase engineered by the International Monetary Fund—left Russia's economy in dire straits. In the early 2000s, newly elected President Vladimir Putin began enacting crucial economic reforms. Along with establishing a semblance of property rights law—a revolutionary reform for that once communist nation—the Russian government instituted a 13% flat income tax.

The effects were instantaneous. In the first year under the Flat Tax, government revenue increased by a whopping 25%, accounting for inflation, and rose again by the same percentage in 2002. By the end of 2004, revenue had more than doubled. Russia claims more billionaires than any country except the U.S., China, Germany, and India. As one publication put it, "Russia is a good place to be if you are rich." Russian president Vladimir Putin savored worldwide publicity when international star Gérard Depardieu, disgusted with France's 75% tax under socialist President François Hollande, chucked his French passport and embraced Russian citizenship. (That extremely unpopular tax has since been abandoned because not only Depardieu but others also left the country.)

Within the last several years, Russia's Flat Tax has faced a number of challenges. The nation's oil-based economy has been wobbling as a result of falling fuel prices and the weakening of the ruble. Unfortunately, politicians in Russia are no different than elsewhere. There has been at least one proposal by the center-left Fair Russia party to impose a 30% tax on high earners. But so far that hasn't happened and Russia is still sticking with its Flat Tax.

Estonia: An Entrepreneurial Powerhouse

Along with its fellow Baltic nations Lithuania and Latvia, Estonia achieved independence in 1991 with the fall of the Soviet Union and was the first to enact a Flat Tax. Its 26% Flat Tax on business and personal incomes proved so successful that, less than a decade later, the country's economy had become the second-fastest growing in Europe, after neighboring Latvia, which also instituted a Flat Tax (see the next section).

Unlike Russia, which has toyed with adding a second tax rate, Estonia understands the importance of keeping a single low tax rate and has, in fact, reduced it to 20%. Estonia also flattened the corporate income tax, which made the country an investment destination for foreign investors.

This fiscal discipline and a sane regulatory environment—Estonia ranks high on the Heritage Foundation/Wall Street Journal Index of Economic Freedom—have helped turn the tiny nation into a magnet for entrepreneurship and global capital. Estonia drew nearly $1 billion in foreign investment in 2014 alone, according to the State Department. Estonia has more start-ups per capita than any European state and has become something of a high-tech hothouse. Skype, for instance, got its start there. Wi-Fi is almost always free. The country has been a model of "e-government." Citizens can file their income taxes and register businesses online and access a wide range of government data.

Estonia's success demonstrates the power of the Flat Tax not only to turn around an economy but also to reduce the size of government. That's precisely why it irks Keynesians like Paul Krugman. In 2012 he enraged Estonians by sniping at the tiny nation for an "incomplete recovery" from the global economic crisis.

Estonia along with its two Baltic neighbors had been hammered when the crisis hit in 2008. But unlike Greece, Italy, Spain, and Portugal, its government slammed on the fiscal brakes. No Keynesian stimulus programs for them. Estonia cut civil servants' salaries 10% and the pay of its government ministers 20%. The Baltic nations rapidly recovered.

Nonetheless, Krugman belittled the successful program Estonia had put in place. As Dan Mitchell deftly pointed out on Forbes.com, Krugman "was guilty of cherry-picking" his data, focusing on the country's failure at the time to return to its GDP level in 2007, while ignoring its spectacular growth since the mid-1990s. Estonians had choice words for the former Princeton professor. President Toomas Ilves, taking to Twitter, called the *New York Times* columnist "smug, overbearing and patronizing"—in addition to some language better left untranslated. The fireworks inspired Latvian composer Eugene Birman to immortalize the feud in *Nostra Culpa*, a 16-minute "financial opera" that debuted in 2013 in Tallinn, the Estonian capital. Birman told an interviewer that the clash merited an opera because it was about more than the Flat Tax. President Ilves was seen as defending his nation's honor. As Estonia's president and citizens saw it, "Professor Krugman was pontificating on a matter that he had no authority to discuss, but this has worked for us and we're not so much interested in what you have to say."

While Europe continues to struggle, Estonia chugs forward.

Latvia: Inflation Nosedives

Just like its Baltic neighbors, Latvia experienced a debilitating economic crisis following the collapse of the Soviet Union, including inflation as high as 958% in 1992. But Latvia was one of the earliest proponents of the Flat Tax, instituting the policy in 1995. Personal income in Latvia is taxed at 23%, and corporate income and capital gains are taxed at 15%.

Since implementing the Flat Tax, Latvia has grown at a rate that is often the fastest in the European Union. Latvia averaged a blistering pace of more than 7% growth from 1996 through 2007, and it is recovering well from the global financial crisis, growing at the respectable rate of about 4% since 2011.

Remember that enormous 958% rate of inflation? It was down to a paltry (by comparison) 25% by 1995, thanks to pro-growth policies. By 2014, Latvia, which has adopted the euro, had an inflation rate of less than 1%.

Lithuania: One of the Fastest-Growing States in the European Union

Like many other former Soviet satellite states, Lithuania began the 1990s with a rough start. Incomes were depressed, and rigid Communist market structures were slow to change into a free market system. Lithuania initially instituted a Flat Tax rate of 33% in 1994, alongside a corporate rate of 15%. It has since decreased the rate to 15% across the board, which has created even greater economic opportunity. Like most countries, Lithuania experienced a sharp, temporary downturn in growth during the global recession. But it has since rebounded and is one of the fastest-growing nations in the European Union.

Hungary: Flat Tax Newcomer

Envious of the growth rates of Flat Tax nations like Estonia, Hungary instituted a 16% Flat Tax in January of 2011. With corporate taxes under 20%, little wonder that the nation's economy, which was contracting, instantly began to revive, reaching a high of 4% growth in 2014. Things have gone so well that the country will lower its rate to 15% in 2016.

Romania: A Flat Tax Helps Create a First-Time Middle Class

Like most other Eastern European nations, Romania had an overly complex tax code that involved five separate rates as high as 40%. The result was a "gray economy" that accounted for an estimated one-third of the nation's economic activity. That all began to change for the better in 2004, when Traian Băsescu won the presidency after running on a Flat Tax platform.

Immediately after taking office, President Băsescu instituted a 16% Flat Tax on individual and business income. Just two years later, economic growth averaged an astounding 7.8% rate over the three-year period between 2006 to 2008. Although Romania, like the rest of the world, was slammed by the global financial crisis, it has since rebounded, thanks to a continuing commitment to pro-growth policies. The Flat Tax has helped attract investment—$3.2 billion last year—that is enabling Romania to create a new middle class and finally move beyond its days of bleak poverty.

The Republic of Georgia: Unstoppable Despite War and the Great Recession

Georgia joined the global Flat Tax fraternity in December 2004, passing the Flat Tax into law by a large margin. Its 12% single rate replaced a confusing multiple-rate system, reducing the size of the tax code by 95%. The economy shot up from less than 6% growth to more than 12% in 2007. There appeared to be no stopping the Georgian economy on its breathtaking upward trajectory. Then came the financial crisis and the Russian invasion of Georgia in 2008, which caused South Ossetia and Abkhazia to break away and become Russian satellites. Such setbacks would be enough to hobble less resilient nations. But Georgia's robust economy stumbled only briefly, suffering just one year of negative growth, in 2009, before rising quickly back to pre-recession growth levels almost immediately, to more than 6% in 2010.

• • •

Of course, a Flat Tax cannot fully insulate a nation from turmoil in the global economy. Every country suffered from the financial panic of 2008 and 2009. But countries with a simple tax system almost always fared better than those with a progressive tax code. For example, compare the fate of Greece with neighboring Macedonia and Bulgaria. Greece's progressive tax system has rates going up to 42%. For this reason and others Greece has been in a semi-depression for several years. By contrast, Bulgaria and Macedonia each have a simple 10% Flat Tax. While Greece's economy contracts, theirs are showing positive growth rates.

The successes of the Flat Tax, however, are not always enough to overcome determined political adversaries. As happens so often, ideology and politics trump reality. Albania and Slovakia are two countries that abandoned the Flat Tax because of left-wing opposition.

Economic growth reached 7.5% after Albania implemented a Flat Tax of 10% in 2008. After the Socialists triumphed in the country's 2013 elections, Albania replaced its Flat Tax with a tiered system with rates as high as 23%. They've paid the price: economic growth under their "progressive" system has slowed to a glacial pace of about 2%.

Slovakia also showed great promise as a model for the Flat Tax. That country replaced an exceedingly complex tax code that included, among other features, five tax brackets, some 90 different exemptions, and two different VATs. In 2003, the Slovak parliament enacted a Flat Tax of 19%. The new tax climate led to a dramatic increase in foreign investment, especially from auto manufacturers like Hyundai-Kia. The *New York Times* dubbed Slovakia "The Detroit of Europe." Then in 2013, Slovakia's newly elected leftist government ditched the Flat Tax in favor of a "directly progressive income tax" with higher rates. In 2014, economic growth was only 2.4%.

Both countries however, are outliers. As one story after another makes clear: the Flat Tax is far and away the best solution for an ailing economy.

Why the Flat Tax
Is a Better Alternative
than a Consumption Tax

W ITH THE ARRIVAL OF THE 2016 ELECTION SEASON, every GOP candidate has proposed some form of tax simplification. Their plans fall into one of three categories:

Traditionalists

Traditionalists want to simplify the current system and lower rates. Jeb Bush wants to reduce the seven brackets now in place to three low tax rates, of 28%, 25%, and 10%. Bush would close some loopholes and the highest rate would return to what it was in the Reagan era. The corporate tax rate would be slashed from 35% to 20%.

Marco Rubio has proposed a plan with two rates, 15% and 35%. That 35% isn't much lower than the 39.6% top rate we have under the Obama administration. Its pro-growth measures include a cut in the corporate tax rate from 35% to 25%. Rubio's plan eliminates the capital gains tax and personal income taxes on dividends and interest. There's also full expensing of business investment and no more taxes on business income already taxed abroad. Like the Bush plan, Rubio would send the Death Tax to the grave.

Chris Christie advocates a Reagan-style plan based on three rates, with a top rate of 28%. He also wants to lower the corporate rate to 25% and encourage corporations to repatriate overseas profits with a low, one-time levy of 8.75%.

Donald Trump's plan has personal three tax rates—10%, 20%, and 25%. Trump gives high exemptions to individuals and married couples. His 15% rate for business income is the lowest among the candidates.

But unlike any other Republican proposal, Trump does not allow for instant expensing of capital outlays and immediately taxes businesses for overseas profits whether they are left abroad or repatriated to the U.S. Under the current code, American corporations pay no tax until profits are brought home. However, under Trump's plan, businesses would still get a credit on foreign taxes paid when computing what they owe Uncle Sam.

All of these plans would be a vast improvement over what we have now. But as we explained earlier, the problem with multiple tax brackets—even when they're low—is that they tend to multiply like rabbits. Ronald Reagan's two rates turned to seven in the Big Government era of Barack Obama.

Flat Taxers

Retired pediatric neurosurgeon Dr. Ben Carson is the only candidate to propose a Flat Tax modeled on the Biblical tithe, only a little bit higher. Senator Ted Cruz has a full-blown plan that would cover both income and payroll taxes. His plan's personal tax rate is 10% and its business tax, similar to Rand Paul's (see below), is 16%. A family of four would pay no federal or payroll tax on their first $36,000 of income.

Former senator Rick Santorum is proposing a Flat Tax of 20% that would retain deductions for charitable contributions and home mortgage interest. The latter would be capped at $25,000. There would be a refundable credit of $2,750 per adult and dependent. This credit, however, cannot exceed the tax filer's earned income. A unique wrinkle would provide manufacturing companies with a 100% income exemption that would phase out over 2 years. Like many other GOP candidates, Santorum would kill the Death Tax.

Libertarian Rand Paul offers a variation of the Flat Tax that he calls "The Fair and Flat Tax." It establishes a 14.5% flat rate tax, applied to all personal income, including wages, salaries, dividends, capital gains, rents, and interest. His plan eliminates the payroll tax on workers and also does away with federal levies on gifts, estates, and telephones. All duties and tariffs are ditched as well. There would be no deductions except for mortgages and charitable giving. The first $50,000 of income for a family of four would not be taxed. For low-income working families, the plan would retain the earned income tax credit.

The fly in the ointment is the second part of Paul's plan, his proposed "business activity tax," a uniform 14.5% consumption tax on companies. In his words, the tax "would be levied on revenues minus allowable expenses, such as the purchase of parts, computers and office equipment. All capital purchases would be immediately expensed, ending complicated depreciation schedules." Tax analyst Dan Mitchell rightly points out that Paul's business activity tax is a version of the dreaded Value-Added Tax (VAT), the consumption-based levy that has been used to expand European social welfare states.

Fair Taxers

With his business activity consumption tax, Rand Paul also has a foot in this camp. Mike Huckabee, however, is the most vigorous advocate of the Fair Tax, also known as the National Retail Sales

Tax. This scheme would place a 30% levy on all services and new products. It replaces personal and corporate income taxes, payroll taxes, the Death Tax, and taxes on savings. This national sales tax would be very much like state and local sales taxes.

Two categories of transaction would be exempt: business-to-business transactions and sales of used goods. That exclusion of B-to-B transactions is the prime difference between the Fair Tax and a European-style VAT. In Europe, the VAT—whose fans include Big Government statists like Barack Obama—exists *in addition* to an income tax and countless other levies.

Over the years the Fair Tax has garnered support from some conservatives, including a number in Congress. Like Flat Tax supporters, they want drastic tax reform and they loathe the IRS. Their hearts are clearly in the right place.

There are a number of challenges, however, that make its implementation very problematical for the foreseeable future. For starters, take the rate: Fair Tax advocates advertise a 23% rate. In reality, the rate is 30%.

Let us explain. Under a Fair Tax, if an item costs $10, you would pay a $3 sales tax. That's 30%. But Fair Tax proponents do the math differently. They add the $10 price to the $3 sales tax. That comes to $13. They then divide the $13 into the $3 sales tax to get their 23% rate. Why advertise 23% instead of the actual 30%? Advocates have their convoluted theories. But the bottom line is the higher rate is a harder sell.

Imagine paying a 30% tax on most products and services. *Thirty percent.* Fair Tax supporters may call this fair. But many consumers will have another word: *Ouch!* That 30% rate presents immediate political problems.

This sleight of hand is far from the only problem with the Fair Tax. In addition to its regressiveness, there are many other equally compelling reasons why this would-be reform is a really bad idea, one that would make the tax system infinitely more painful and complicated than it is today.

Tax reformers who think a Fair Tax is the way to go should consider these major drawbacks:

The Fair Tax would be especially unfair to poor people. A 30% sales tax would be painful enough for the average American. But it would be even harder on the poor, many of whom right now don't pay income taxes. More than 43% of American households paid no tax in 2013. Many would be crushed by a 30% tax that would make many basic consumer items, including necessities like groceries, unaffordable.

Convoluted welfare-like refunds known as "prebates" that everyone would receive. Fair Tax proponents, concerned by the likelihood of resistance to their plan's regressive 30% rate, soften the sting of their levy with a scheme known as "prebates." Each month, Washington would issue every household a check to offset the tax levied on necessities, directed especially to those families below the poverty line. According to FairTax.org:

> This is not an entitlement, but a rebate (in advance) of taxes paid—thus the term prebate . . . For example, a two adult/two child family spending at the poverty level has a 0% effective tax rate because the annual prebate of $7,328 refunds all of the taxes they pay on their annual spending of $31,860.

Prebates are *unfair* because you'd get the same dollar amount whether you live in an expensive city or a rural area with a low cost of living. In other words, Fair Tax refunds favor people in rural areas over the struggling urban poor. This is a serious drawback when you consider that 13 million people live in poverty in America's cities.

Implementing the Fair Tax would require a new costly bureaucracy. All taxpayers regardless of income would get the prebate—not only low-income people but also wealthy Americans. Processing and dispensing these government checks would require an enormous bureaucracy. How wasteful is *that?* All that money and manpower for a massive government apparatus to refund money that shouldn't have been taken in the first place. The cost of a prebate program has been estimated to be as high as $543 billion.

Then there's the issue of just which government bureaucracies would collect these taxes. Right now sales taxes are collected by the states. Each state has different laws regarding what can be taxed, not to mention different rates—and five states have no sales tax at all.

Fair Tax advocates maintain that the states would do the job since most already have sales tax collection machinery. As an incentive, they would keep one-quarter of 1% of the Fair Tax revenues they gather. But who would audit *the states* to make sure Uncle Sam gets his cut?

The Fair Tax Would Be Susceptible to Tax Evasion.   Experience shows that sales taxes present major enforcement problems when rates go beyond 10%. The Fair Tax places retailers in the unpleasant position of having to act as proxies for the federal government, policing their customers in order to collect the tax. They'd have to determine, for example, whether lumber just purchased was intended for a business purpose (and is thus exempt from the tax) or whether it will be used for the taxable purpose of fixing a customer's kitchen. How many retailers are likely to risk irking their customers with such intrusive queries? And, again, what government entities will determine which business is legitimate and which is a sham?

Fair Tax advocates are kidding themselves if they think there wouldn't be resistance to this idea. The result would be an enormous "gray" economy designed with the sole purpose of helping consumers avoid paying an outrageous tax. Again, any "business exemption" to a sales tax would create a rush of people forming fake businesses. After all, if you can avoid a 30% tax hike by forming an LLC and conducting every transaction through that channel, why wouldn't you? Not only would such false businesses cause problems, they would create a hostile and suspicious regulatory environment for real businesses.

Services would be especially vulnerable to evasion. Fair Tax advocates claim that this exaction would be harder to avoid than the income tax. Really? A mechanic fixes your car. You pay in cash. With a 30% tax, there would be all sorts of schemes and evasions that would be extremely hard to track.

There's another wrinkle: What is "new"? Take a house. A new one that sold for $200,000 would be hit with a $60,000 tax. An entrepreneurial builder *totally* remodels an existing house so that it's brand new in all but name. Is it taxed or not? And, once more, who makes that determination?

Or how about a car? Sometimes dealers will cut the price of a new vehicle that has been used for demo drives. Is that vehicle really new or not?

What about car leases? You might pony up the 30% on the lease payments. Then you turn the car in and the dealer sells it. Is that sale exempt from the tax? And what if you buy it? It's old, so is it tax-free? The answers might lead to only leases being used in auto sales, which would cut projected sales tax revenues.

A vivid example of what happens when consumption taxes are too high: New York's state and city taxes on cigarettes, the highest in the nation, which bring the cost of a pack to more than $14.

Result: over half the cigarettes sold in New York City are bootlegs, imported from Native American reservations or low-tax states. The business is so lucrative that sellers will even create cigarette packages that have tax stamps that look like the real thing.

Compliance gets even more complicated. Retailers, like the states, would get a quarter of 1% incentive to collect the tax. But the steep additional administrative costs—especially for small retailers like boutique stores—would raise the temptation to cut corners. And let's not forget that there are nearly 10,000 sales tax jurisdictions in the United States. What federal government agency is going to oversee all of these to make sure they are in compliance?

And what about the Internet? A lot of Washington politicians are already pushing legislation that would crush small e-commerce retailers with a hideously complex scheme to have them collect sales taxes no matter where their customers live. The software doesn't yet exist that enables small entities to cope with the filings for thousands of jurisdictions. Only the biggest players like Amazon could likely absorb the extra costs. The Internet owes its growth to its status as a lightly regulated market largely free of taxes. By taking away this competitive advantage, the Fair Tax would hurt companies that have been one of the economy's few bright spots in the past several years.

Fraud would be rampant. The prebate program would also be highly susceptible to fraud, like every government agency that collects or disburses funds. Do we want another bureaucracy with the potential to be defrauded like the Social Security Administration? That rip-off-riddled agency managed to issue a staggering $7.9 billion in improper or fraudulent benefits in 2012. The SSA's Old-Age, Survivors, and Disability Insurance payments alone accounted for $1.9 billion in erroneous payments in 2013. Even the IRS has problems with refunds. The tax agency issued 23,994 checks totaling $46,378,040 to *a single address* in Atlanta, Georgia in 2011.

In this age of endemic hacking, the problem of fraud should not be minimized.

The Fair Tax would be a major drain on the economy. The Fair Tax would be as harsh on the economy as it would be on individuals. We mentioned how it would harm e-commerce, a major source of job growth. But it would hurt other critical sectors, too. To take another example, let's go back to that 30% tax on the price of new homes. What would happen to the market for new houses? Homebuyers are a critical driver of economic growth, but this tax would put home ownership outside the reach of many prospective homebuyers and push the market exclusively to homes built before the passage of the tax.

Despite its exemption for business-to-business transactions, many businesses will end up paying the tax despite the B-to-B exemption, as happens now with sales taxes. When a company buys, for instance, a sheet of steel, it's not supposed to pay sales tax on that material. But, according to one estimate, about 40% of state sales taxes fall improperly on business inputs.

The Fair Tax is especially unfair in a down economy. That's because you always have to pay a 30% Fair Tax on what you buy, regardless of how much you happen to be earning. Even the current system affords you a reprieve if you've lost your job and your income drops to zero. But with the Fair Tax, you'd have to pay that 30% on your mortgage and other essentials during a recession when you may be earning less and least able to afford it. How fair is that?

The Fair Tax opens the door to a new entitlement. A national sales tax would be subject to the same kind of meddling and manipulation that has corrupted the current taxation system. The prebate program is especially vulnerable. There would be political pressure to increase these payouts and to differentiate between people of various incomes. It would be far too easy for the Fair Tax to evolve into a gigantic new entitlement.

The Fair Tax regime will become a political football like the current tax code. The Fair Tax plan exempts college tuition payments from the 30% sales tax. Smart politics, seemingly. But this opens the door to countless other seemingly worthy or politically potent exceptions, starting with what we discussed earlier, new houses.

The Fair Tax has rosy revenue assumptions. Advocates want to apply this levy to government purchases of products and services to make their tax receipt estimates work. That means that when the Pentagon buys an aircraft carrier for, say, $10 billion, it will fork over another $3 billion in sales taxes to the Treasury Department. Good luck with that. Local school districts that buy textbooks and other educational tools will be paying that 30% tax? Imagine how local property taxpayers and parents will react. Politically, that's a non-starter.

A Fair Tax would require repeal of the 16th Amendment to the Constitution. In 1895, the Supreme Court ruled that the Constitution doesn't give the federal government the authority to enact an income tax. The subsequent 16th Amendment overruled that decision, granting Congress the "power to lay and collect taxes on incomes, from whatever source derived, without apportionment among the several States, and without regard to any census or enumeration." If this amendment is not repealed, then the U.S. will suffer the fate of most nations and be saddled with both an income and a consumption tax. By the way, that condition holds in most American states today—they have both an income and a sales tax.

   If you really want to replace the income tax with the Fair Tax you must repeal the 16th Amendment, and that would have to pass both houses of Congress by a two-thirds vote. Even if the amendment passed in Congress, it would then have to be ratified by 38 out of 50 states. There's a good reason why there have been relatively few constitutional amendments.

Why go through so much trouble when the Flat Tax can be easily implemented via the normal legislative process? The Flat Tax will accomplish all the goals desired by Fair Tax advocates and then some—without added costs and layers of government. It will make more efficient use of the revenue collection methods we have in place, dramatically shrinking Washington's tax bureaucracy. The Flat Tax would not increase but drastically reduce opportunities for tax avoidance. And the simple mechanics of the system would sharply decrease incentives for fraud. Finally, the Flat Tax would not impose a regressive burden on consumers that needs to be softened with a "prebate." It would instead bring true tax fairness, enabling hundreds of millions of people to keep more of their earnings, for themselves and their families. And it would let them invest this wealth to create opportunities, which would benefit all of us. Now *that's* fair.

CHAPTER 8

Why Flat Tax Critics
Are Flat Out Wrong

THE FLAT TAX HAS WORKED IN SCORES OF ECONOMIES. But, as with any new idea, there are always doubters unable or unwilling to acknowledge the facts. In the case of the Flat Tax, naysayers have come up with every objection imaginable. They insist the Flat Tax will harm charitable giving, home ownership, fiscal soundness in Washington, municipal bonds, healthcare—everything except the kitchen sink. They'll tell you that the Flat Tax hurts the poor and unfairly favors the "1%." To see why these criticisms are flat out wrong, you only need to look at the facts. Here are some of the most pervasive Flat Tax myths:

Myth: *The Flat Tax hurts the poor.*
Reality: *The Flat Tax is fairer than today's "progressive" tax code.*

The Flat Tax would help, not hurt, the poor. As we explain in Chapter 5, the exemptions offered under the Flat Tax are far more generous than those under the current tax code—$13,200 for each adult and child compared with a measly $4,000 under the present system. Right now the standard deductions are $6,300 for an individual and $12,600 for a married couple. Remember, under a Flat Tax a family of four with $52,800 or less in income *would pay no*

93

federal income taxes. Under the current code, that total exemption is a pitiful $28,600.

The Flat Tax would also allow low-income Americans to save on the cost of tax preparation. Even if they don't pay income taxes, low income earners still need to go through the expense of filing a return under our current system. This hurts them because they pay a higher percent of their income for tax preparation than higher earning people—4.5%. Being able to fill out a card or a brief form via computer would put much-needed money back in their pockets.

Under a Flat Tax, low-income people would also be able to get refunds without having to complete the complicated paperwork required to qualify for the Earned Income Tax Credit.

Finally, they would benefit from the vitality of a Flat Tax economy. Just as it has in other countries, the Flat Tax will usher in an era of American Revival and history-making prosperity. Low-income earners would find it easier to move up the ladder because of access to more and better jobs and opportunities.

Myth: *The Flat Tax benefits the wealthy.*
Reality: *It benefits everybody.*

The Flat Tax is a tax cut for everyone. Not only that, it would abolish the tax breaks that so enrage liberals. No more finagling complicated rules and deductions. Such loopholes wouldn't exist. The Flat Tax would make it harder for high-income people and businesses to game the system with the help of expensive tax lawyers or lobbyists. Everyone would be playing by the same rules.

The rich would end up contributing more to Uncle Sam's income tax revenue under a Flat Tax. High taxes traditionally push high earners to shelter income. But when taxes are cut, there is less incentive to engage in tax-avoidance strategies. Moreover, since success is no longer punished, people have more capital to invest. High-income entrepreneurs and job creators would end up paying more in taxes. That is precisely what happened in the aftermath of the Reagan tax cuts. Prior to the passage of those cuts in 1981, the top 1% of American earners accounted for nearly 18% of federal personal income tax revenue. By 1988, that same group accounted for nearly 28%, an increase of 10 percentage points in only 7 years. Isn't that the kind of "fairness" liberals want?

Myth: *The Flat Tax will hurt charitable giving.*
Reality: *Charitable giving would increase with a Flat Tax.*

Some commentators worry that, by eliminating deductions, a Flat Tax would drastically reduce charitable donations. The opposite is true: a Flat Tax would spur an *increase* in charitable giving. The reason is as simple as the Flat Tax itself: charitable giving surges during a strong economy. Research from Stanford University (see the chart in Figure 8.1) shows the strong correlation between giving and economic growth. From 1995 to 2007, overall a period of prosperity, charitable giving rose sharply. There was one notable decline—during the 2000–2001 downturn. No surprise, in 2008, according to researchers, total giving plunged by 7% in inflation-adjusted dollars, from $326.6 billion

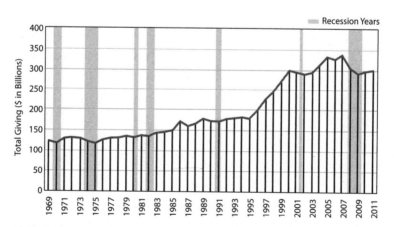

FIGURE 8.1   *Total charitable giving (inflation adjusted dollars).*
Source: *GivingUSA Foundation*

to $303.8 billion. In 2009, it dropped another 6.2% to approximately $284.9 billion.

As Figure 8.1 so clearly shows, all the deductions in the world won't help charitable giving in a down economy, when people have less to give away. And there's another little known reality: a substantial portion of giving isn't deducted. According to the Committee for a Responsible Federal Budget, nearly $300 billion was donated to 1.1 million charities in 2011. But only $175 billion of that was deducted as a charitable contribution. The rest was donated by non-itemizers who did not claim the deduction.

Throughout our history, Americans have consistently given generously to charity without consideration of tax breaks. Witness the tremendous outpourings of generosity following events like 9/11, Hurricane Katrina, the tsunami in southeast Asia, and even the "Ice Bucket Challenge," that raised awareness and research funding for Lou Gehrig's disease, which generated $115 million for the ALS Association in a six-week period in 2014.

Americans' cash contributions to charities have always been roughly 2% of GDP. In hard times this number might fall to 1.8%. When the economy is booming it might rise to 2.2%. What this goes to show is the point we frequently make, when Americans have more, they give more.

Additional evidence comes from examining responses to changes in the tax code. In the last 35 years, Congress has substantially altered the tax code several times—in 1981, 1986, and 2003. The changes involved substantial cuts in individual rates. In 2001, Congress passed legislation to phase out the Death Tax. Each time taxes were cut, people expressed concerns that lowering tax rates would reduce philanthropy. But every time they were wrong.

Take the most dramatic example from the 1980s: When the top personal rate was slashed from 70% to 28%, many philanthropic organizations opposed the reduction. They feared a drop in donations because Washington's tax breaks were being sharply cut. To the contrary, from 1980 to 1989, individual donations grew at an annual rate of 5.2%.

Myth: *The Flat Tax would deplete the Treasury.*
Reality: *It eventually means more revenue for government.*

Statists who like to punish "the rich" hate the idea of lowering taxes. So, they're especially spooked by the idea of a Flat Tax providing massive tax relief. Washington bean counters worry that there won't be enough revenue for government programs.

The belief that lower taxes produce lower income tax receipts is based on Washington's method of economic forecasting, which relies on a methodology known as *static analysis*. It predicts the future based on conditions in the present. Static analysis is flawed because it doesn't take into account how people *react* to change— in this case, the lowering of taxes. Predictions that lowering taxes will in turn lower revenues ignore the historic effects of tax cuts on people and markets: when tax rates come down, capital that would have been diverted by the IRS is invested in entrepreneurial job-creating ventures, and spent on products that further boost the economy.

To demonstrate the absurdity of the government's thinking, we pose the question: How much would you want to work if you were taxed at 100%? The likely answer is, not very much. Why work if government is going to keep all of your money?

The answer would seem like a no-brainer to everyone, that is, except Washington bureaucrats. In 1988, Senator Robert Packwood (R-OR), then ranking Republican on the Finance Committee, asked the Congressional Joint Committee on Taxation to assess the impact on revenue if government confiscated all income over $200,000 annually. The committee's number cruncher predicted this would raise $104 billion the first year, $204 billion the second year, $232 billion the third year, and $263 billion and $299 billion in the fourth and fifth years, respectively.

Their forecast was based on the remarkable assumption that people would continue to work *even if the government confiscated all of their salary*. To say this defies common sense is something of an understatement.

The CBO predicted that the 1986 increase in the capital gains levy would raise more revenue. They were spectacularly mistaken. Federal collections fell from about $53 billion in 1986 to $34 billion in 1987.

By contrast, when the capital gains rate was reduced in 1981 from 28% to 20%, the CBO predicted a fall in revenue. Instead, from 1981 to 1986, federal receipts almost quadrupled. When this exaction was cut in 1997 and even further in 2003, revenues went up immediately.

Although the capital gains levy would be eliminated under a Flat Tax, the point here is that lowering taxes, regardless of which levies they are, produces an increase in activity and, ultimately, tax receipts. Government revenues, however, will initially fall when the Flat Tax is enacted. It takes time for increased business investment to take place and pay off.

Static analysis has failed so often it's a wonder that anyone gives it credence. The reality is that the federal government has consistently and grossly underestimated tax receipts resulting

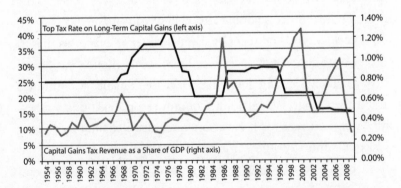

FIGURE 8.2 *Periods of high capital gains tax rates produce less revenue.*
Source: *U.S. Treasury*

from tax cuts and overestimated the windfalls that result from tax increases. It's time to wake up and look at the historical realities and the successes of countries that have implemented a Flat Tax.

Myth: *The Flat Tax would slow or stop job creation.*
Reality: *It would create jobs.*

Some critics have insisted that by allowing instant write-offs for capital investment, the Flat Tax would encourage companies to invest in equipment and other assets at the expense of hiring new employees. This convoluted argument has been made against other pro-business tax cuts, such as President George W. Bush's 2003 capital gains tax cut. What happened was the opposite: the cuts produced a miniboom. Unemployment immediately began to drop, from around 6% to a low of 4.4% in 2006, before the financial crisis.

Such critics fail to fully understand that the Flat Tax is a fundamental change in the tax code. Its low single rate creates a permanent investment incentive. Businesses wouldn't need to rush to invest in equipment because the Flat Tax is not a political gimmick like a credit or a temporary cut that eventually disappears.

A Flat Tax would permit full, immediate write-offs of business capital spending. Buy a $100,000 piece of machinery and you'd have a $100,000 expense for tax purposes. Any losses could be carried forward to offset future profits.

No longer would business owners be faced with a fluctuating tax code that forces them to read the tea leaves to figure out if they will be punished next year for a decision they would be rewarded for this year.

This change would unleash a flood of new investment into plant and equipment. But it would also mean countless new jobs. After all, you need people to operate all that machinery.

Not every Flat Tax concern is a myth. Once the mechanics of the system are fully explained, however, the anxieties usually evaporate. Below, some common questions answered.

Q: *Wouldn't I lose my mortgage deduction?*
A: *Yes. But this "loss" will be more than offset by your gain under a Flat Tax.*

The anxiety about the mortgage interest deduction is understandable. Millions of Americans each year deduct interest payments on their home mortgages from their taxable income to lower their tax bill. As we've explained, under a Flat Tax, there are no deductions after the personal exemptions. So yes, you would "lose" the deduction for mortgage interest. But this "loss" would be more than offset by what you'd gain.

Remember, the Flat Tax itself will be a tax cut. You will already be paying less.

This reduction would more than cover the loss of exemptions for mortgage interest and property taxes. In other words, *the taxes saved would be greater than the deductions.*

But the gain doesn't end there. Here's something else opponents of the Flat Tax won't tell you: the Flat Tax would lower interest rates by about 20% in a normal interest rate environment. Economists and Flat Tax architects Robert Hall and Alvin Rabushka, who did their groundbreaking work at Stanford University's Hoover Institution, have explained that, under a Flat Tax, lenders would no longer have to pay tax on interest revenue from borrowers. Because the Flat Tax would lower the cost of lending, rates therefore would drop.

This is not theoretical. Municipal bond income is free from federal taxation and, for residents, from state income taxes. A Flat Tax means that homeowners would get similar "muni" treatment. Other experts have confirmed Hall and Rabushka's findings.

The homebuilding industry is also concerned about losing the mortgage interest deduction because they fear it would hurt home sales. Again, not true. Under a Flat Tax, you would see higher personal incomes. That would bring with it the ability to buy a better house. In a vibrant economy people buy either a bigger home or remodel their existing one. Add in lower interest rates on mortgages as well as on other loans and you have the ingredients for a very happy homebuilding industry.

Remember, for those who are still unconvinced, taxpayers will have a choice between going to a Flat Tax—or staying with the old convoluted system.

Q: *Won't the Flat Tax cause people to stop buying tax-free municipal bonds—hurting the cities and towns that rely on them?*
A: *No. There will still be a market for them. But the quality of the investments will matter more.*

Critics claim that, because the Flat Tax would make all bonds tax-free, investors would no longer be motivated to put money into the lower-interest municipal bonds cities and towns rely on to build schools, roads, and other infrastructure. Not true. In a tax-free environment, people would still buy municipal bonds. But investors would pay more attention to credit quality and what the money is actually being used for. State and local governments would have to improve the quality of their projects to attract investors, since they couldn't simply lure them with tax advantages. This would mean fewer white elephant projects, like sports stadiums, and more responsible fiscal policies.

As for your own bond portfolio, a Flat Tax would render all bond interest tax-free. You'd be able to continue to receive your tax-free muni interest payments and the value of these bonds would not be affected. The only change with a Flat Tax is that, assuming no change in the interest rate environment, the value of your corporate and Treasury bonds would go up, since their interest would be free from federal income taxes.

Q: *Won't I lose deductions for state and local taxes?*
A: *Yes. But, once again, the federal tax cut makes up for it.*

As with mortgage interest, the Flat Tax will lower taxes overall so substantially that you'll never miss those deductions. There's also another secondary benefit. Doing away with state and local tax deductions will increase the pressure on local governments to cut their rates. Feeling increased pain from local taxes, taxpayers in high-tax cities and states would push for lower rates. This happened after Reagan slashed the top federal rate to 28% in 1986. Several states, including New York, reduced their rates.

Q: *What happens to tax-free benefits like IRAs and health savings accounts?*
A: *A Flat Tax is compatible with HSAs and IRAs. And it would make healthcare more affordable.*

What if companies no longer get a deduction for providing benefits like health insurance—or, for that matter, individual retirement accounts? Would they continue to provide them?

The answer is yes. Employers were offering health insurance, as we explained in the first part of this book, before they received a tax deduction for it. Even without a tax break, some companies may continue to offer some form of health insurance in order to attract and retain employees in a fiercely competitive labor market, which will develop when the economy rapidly grows again. Further, a Flat Tax would make it easier to offer such benefits because it would dramatically lower the levies that have helped inflate the cost of healthcare and insurance premiums.

What about IRAs and other retirement vehicles? Many employers will continue to offer them for the same reason they'll continue to offer health insurance. But, under a Flat Tax, the IRA of the future would more closely resemble the Roth IRA. Those savings vehicles allow you to set aside after-tax money that can be withdrawn tax-free after the age of 59½. It's a fact of human nature that people find it convenient to own special accounts dedicated for specific purposes. But, in contrast to today, there would be no limits on IRA contributions under the Flat Tax. Companies would likely offer defined contribution plans as a way of attracting employees. In the future these would operate like the Roth IRA.

The Bottom Line

The advantages of the Flat Tax are clear. The Flat Tax would provide tax relief to everyone. Allowing citizens to fill out their return on a single page, it de-clutters today's confused system and frees Americans from the burden of preparing their taxes. The Flat Tax eliminates the power and corruption that have resulted from today's gargantuan tax code. Unlike the Fair Tax, it requires no new bureaucratic apparatus or an amendment to the Constitution. Liberating the economy from today's system of double and even triple taxation, as well as costly compliance, the Flat Tax would unleash a flood of capital, creating an historic boom that would help people across all sectors. Eliminating loopholes and requiring everyone to pay their fair share, it offers a model of tax fairness that is even found in the Bible.

When all the facts are considered, the real question is not whether America should implement this vital reform, but *what are we waiting for?*

REFORM THE FED: No More Soviet-Style Controls over Money and Credit

CHAPTER 9

Why Our Current System of Unstable Money Has Been Part of the Problem

W
HY IS MONEY SO FUNDAMENTALLY IMPORTANT?
Money allows society to advance by facilitating commerce, the buying and selling that enables people to
meet each other's needs. By providing an agreed-upon standard of
value in these transactions, money helps establish trust. That's why,
when money is unable to function as it should, there are repercus-
sions not only for the economy but all of society.

We are seeing this today. Few people can recall a period of
greater uncertainty. The last decade has been witness to the bursting
of a momentous housing bubble, a financial crisis and stock market
panic that began in the U.S. and spread across the world that was
followed by the historically weak recovery. More recently, nerves
have been rattled by a stock market that seems to grow ever more
violent, hitting ever-higher highs, only to take stomach-churning
slides. In August of 2015, for example, the perception of a slowdown in the Chinese economy and the weakening of the yuan sent
the Dow Jones Average down more than 1,000 points. The market
surged before backing down and closing out the third quarter with

107

significant losses. No one would be surprised if another bad piece of economic news hammers stocks yet again.

Every other day, there are new rumors that Greece might default and leave the euro. There have been currency crises in Russia, Turkey, and South Africa. Even the once-impressive Australian dollar has been clobbered. Brazil—which had been one of the few bright spots in South America—suddenly looked more like its perpetually troubled neighbors Argentina and Venezuela as its economy slid into recession. And there's the uncertain Chinese economy, whose fabled growth has sharply slowed.

No surprise, governments everywhere have been turning over. Everyone is on edge. As was the case in the 1930s and 1970s, political leaders appear unable to cope. Voters unnerved by this collapse in leadership are becoming more open to political extremes and outsider candidates—Greece, the U.S., and the United Kingdom are but three examples in 2015. Politicians and ordinary citizens alike complain that the system has become fundamentally unfair. Both left and right are angry about everything from "inequality" to "illegals." Groups like Black Lives Matter stage angry demonstrations, while Baltimore and Ferguson, Missouri erupt in violence.

Few observers recognize that today's violent markets and political disarray are direct results of a monetary system based on a fluctuating dollar. This is why returning to a dollar whose value is linked to gold is the third of our Big Three Reforms needed to revive America and bring back hope.

For most of our history, the U.S. relied on sound money. The dollar was pegged to gold and had a fixed value. Then in 1971 Richard Nixon severed the link to gold, ending the Bretton Woods gold standard that had been in place since the end of World War II and allowing the dollar to float on global currency markets.

We are now living with the destructive consequences of this fateful decision. A study by noted economists from Rutgers University, the University of California at Berkeley, and the World

Bank found that, since the early 1970s, the frequency of major economic crises had *doubled* over what it had been for most of the past 120 years. And that study was conducted in 2000, before the financial crisis, which, as we'll discuss in the coming chapters, would not have occurred had the Fed not weakened the dollar.

Central Planners

The Federal Reserve may be the closest thing we have to a Soviet-style central planning bureaucracy. It tries to control the direction of the economy by raising and lowering interest rates. It does so primarily by engaging in so-called "open market operations," the buying and selling of primarily Treasury securities to expand or reduce the nation's monetary base.

We explain in the following chapter that the Fed was founded originally as a lender of last resort, a source of emergency liquidity for the banking system. Unfortunately, it long ago exceeded this role and is now exerting unprecedented power over banks and, increasingly, other financial institutions. Its command-and-control strategies even include the allocation of credit. This produces distortions you always get with government domination: oversupply and/or shortages.

So how did the Fed grow into the monster we have today? Because today's political establishment has embraced the belief—one that dates back centuries to the mercantilist era—that controlling money is the way to a prosperous economy.

That has never been true. Manipulating the value of money and interest rates never created wealth or sustainable prosperity. Wealth is created by innovation: inventing a new product or technology like the automobile or the iPhone that improves millions of lives. What money does is *measure* wealth, like a clock measures time and a ruler measures space. It is the most important of all society's weights and measures. That's why, to function properly, it should have a fixed value.

We never question the need for *other* fixed weights and measures. No one doubts that it's important for a scale to provide a constant measure of weight. You need to be sure, for instance, that when you buy a pound of cheese, you're getting 16 ounces. Or that the gallon of gasoline you buy is the same quantity as the gallon you bought last week. Nor do we question the necessity of an unchanging 60-minute hour. Without such measures, society couldn't function.

Imagine the confusion that would ensue if the Federal Reserve did to watches and clocks what it does to the dollar. What if the hour fluctuated in value from 60 minutes one day, to 48 the next, to 80 the day after that? Life would be chaotic. How could you bake a cake if a recipe called for "one half hour at 350 degrees"—and you weren't sure if that half hour consisted of 30 minutes or 40? Or how could a school operate if no one could be certain if history class would be given in a 60-minute hour or a 90-minute hour? The uncertainty would paralyze people and organizations.

If the U.S. and global economy is ever to fully rebound, we must return to a monetary system based on a sound dollar. Allow today's destructive policies to continue, and the nation faces a disheartening future of sub-par growth, declining living standards, slowing upward mobility, and growing discontent. America will no longer be a bountiful land of opportunity for people who want to better their lives and improve the prospects of their children and grandchildren. Below, a closer look at the reasons we need reform.

Wealth Destruction and "Stealth Taxation" Resulting from the Unstable Dollar

The Fed's control of money weakens the dollar. The greenback's purchasing power has been debased since Richard Nixon severed the link to gold more than four decades ago, resulting in the Fed-controlled fiat dollar. Amazingly, a dollar today would buy the equivalent of just 17 cents in 1971. This erosion accelerated in the early 2000s. According to the government's Consumer Price Index Inflation Calculator, the dollar's buying power has decreased by 28% since the dollar started weakening fifteen years ago. A dollar in 2015 buys what 72 cents did in 2000.

When the Fed deliberately weakens the dollar to achieve its arbitrary goal of 2% inflation, it is in effect taxing each and every American. Economist John Maynard Keynes, whose ideas are the basis for today's monetary system, famously acknowledged that inflation is a stealth tax whereby "government can confiscate, secretly and unobserved, an important part of the wealth of their citizens." Yet no one ever questions the absurdity and brutality of weak money. The press applauded Fed Chairwoman Janet Yellen when she announced the Fed's goal of creating 2% inflation to "stimulate" the economy. For a family making $50,000 a year, a 2% rise in prices means an additional cost of living of $1,000. How is that supposed to boost the economy?

Political Divisiveness and Destruction of Social Trust

Few of us fully appreciate how important sound money is to social trust. Investment strategist Dylan Grice put it succinctly: "History is replete with Great Disorders in which social cohesion has been undermined by currency debasements." The foremost example of course is the political extremism—the scapegoating of the Jews and the rise of Adolf Hitler—that took place as a result of the German hyperinflation. But similar scenarios are unfolding around the world today. To cite just one: Brazil's currency in 2015 has taken a precipitous fall in value. Serious demonstrations have erupted. Political unrest is seething, with calls for the impeachment of the president.

Even low levels of inflation can undermine trust and promote discord. That's because when the dollar fluctuates, certain segments of the economy reap rewards at the expense of others.

For instance, Wall Street realized enormous gains selling trillions of dollars of government bonds and mortgage-backed securities to the Fed, which bought them with money created out of thin air during the years of Quantitative Easing (QE). Until the dollar strengthened in 2013, commodity producers also received a windfall. That's because, when money is weakened, it typically flows into hard assets like oil, corn, land, and gold.

From the early 2000s to 2013, "the 1%"—wealthy financial industry managers and commodity producers—benefited. Meanwhile "the 99%," savers and people on fixed incomes, saw the value of their money decline. It's no coincidence that in this era "inequality" has emerged as a hot-button issue igniting street demonstrations. People who are struggling get angry when they see others reaping what appear to be excessive and unfair gains. Rising commodity prices also encourage unrest. The demonstrations that set off the Arab Spring, for example, began over soaring food prices.

Fluctuating money destroys trust because it undermines fundamental relationships between buyer and seller, lender and creditor that are vital to social cohesion. The corruption of unstable money is summed up best by John Locke, who famously observed how inflation defrauds both lender and creditor: "Whether the creditor be forced to receive less, or the debtor be forced to pay more than his contract, the damage and injury is the same, whenever a man is defrauded of his due." The recent housing crisis created by the weak dollar was a perfect illustration of Locke's scenario: Lenders were seen as "predatory" and borrowers walked away from their mortgages.

Crime is also associated with this breakdown of trust. Studies have shown that monetary instability correlates with increases in criminal activity. It's no accident that New York and other cities have recently reported increases in violent crime. Many people today see parallels with the high-crime, high-inflation 1970s. The late great economist and journalist Henry Hazlitt observed the relationship between crime and loose money. In his words, "Reward comes to depend less and less on effort and production." Therefore, "corruption or crime [seems] a surer path to quick reward."

Monetary Instability Encourages Domineering Government

Governments respond to the upheaval and turmoil created by unstable money by becoming more coercive. Nations roiled by currency crises impose restraints on bank withdrawals—such as Greece did in 2015—and other strictures aimed at getting chaotic, panicked markets under control. The stock market panic at the height of the financial crisis helped elect the far-left Barack Obama, who enacted sweeping regulations not only on the financial industry but also, as we've seen, on healthcare and other sectors of the economy.

Corrupted Prices and Market Bubbles

A fluctuating dollar corrupts the price system driving the economy. Prices are how markets communicate to producers and consumers. They tell producers which goods and services are needed, and which aren't. High prices with the promise of profits mobilize producers to enter a market and meet the needs and wants of consumers. In the early days of cell phones, high prices attracted producers who flooded the market with new offerings. People got the phones they wanted. And prices came down, too.

When the Fed artificially manipulates the dollar, this system of communication becomes distorted. The market sends producers and consumers erroneous signals. The result is a misallocation of capital and wasted investment that all too often produces commodity bubbles. People uncertain of the future value of their money seek to protect their wealth by investing in commodities and hard assets like gold, oil, copper, and real estate. This artificial rush of dollars is frequently misread as genuine demand.

The classic example is the 1970s energy crisis. Few people then (never mind now) connected the era's soaring fuel prices to the inflation that ensued after Richard Nixon severed the dollar's link to gold. They thought, mistakenly, that we were running out of energy sources.

The "crisis" disappeared after Paul Volcker, Fed Chairman under Ronald Reagan, wrung out inflation and stabilized the dollar. There was no talk of soaring fuel prices or an energy crisis for the rest of the 1980s into the late 1990s, the period known as "The Great Moderation," when there was a largely stable dollar.

Oil prices were again driven skyward by the weak dollar in the early 2000s. This generated a global alternative energy mania: After all, didn't rising prices mean we were running out of oil? Shouldn't governments direct capital towards developing new sources of energy? Germany, for one, responded by spending the equivalent of hundreds of billions of dollars on alternative energy sources. The outcome? Electric bills that are two to three times the rates in the U.S. That's why German chemical companies are building their new facilities over here.

Dollar fluctuations probably account for 80% of commodity price movements. Demand, for example, cannot account for oil plunging to as low as $10 a barrel in 1999 or, in the early 2000s, rocketing from $25 to over $100 a barrel. Yet pundits and politicians, and the general public, are rarely aware of the dollar's role in these market swings.

Increased Speculation and a More Dangerous Global Economy

We mentioned earlier that the unstable dollar has been responsible for a doubling in the occurrence of the major systemic crises that shake the U.S. and the world. The most horrific was the 2008–09 financial crisis, the consequence primarily—though not exclusively—of a housing bubble produced by the weakening of the dollar. Also playing a key role was the reinstatement of mark-to-market accounting rules that caused banks to undervalue their assets.

The stage for this disaster was set in 2001, when the Fed began cutting interest rates and debasing the dollar to combat the recession that had started at the end of the previous year. It continued this so-called easy money policy for too long after the economy had turned around. Officials thought that this would increase exports and stimulate the domestic economy. What it actually did was create a boom in commodities like gold, copper, and soybeans. Housing prices also started to go up.

But the housing bubble of 2001–2007 was different from the inflation-driven surge in housing prices of the 1970s. This time the weak dollar wasn't the only factor. Other stimulants were fueling the mania—namely, the government-sponsored enterprises (GSEs) Fannie Mae and then Freddie Mac. Originating as affordable housing programs and later spun off as public companies, the two GSEs bought mortgages, pooled them together, and then sold the packages to investors. With their implicit guarantee from Uncle Sam, they could borrow at lower rates than private companies. With their vast financial resources, they also became political powerhouses, contributing to political campaigns and employing countless former politicians, their relatives, and staffers. Not surprisingly, Congress turned a blind eye as these entities borrowed vast amounts of money on a scale no private corporation would be able to.

Add to this a Washington political climate fixated on the idea that everyone should have a house, almost without regard to their financial circumstances. Fannie and Freddie actually had quotas for buying sub-prime mortgages. The eventual outcome: a flood of artificial liquidity was pumped into the housing market, producing soaring prices and a housing mania that eventually collapsed. The aftermath afflicts us to this day.

This debacle was widely blamed on Wall Street "greed" and "predatory lending." Few observers even today fully appreciate the role played by the weakening of the dollar during the administrations of both George W. Bush and Barack Obama.

The Disastrous Failure and Global Disruption Caused by Quantitative Easing

If there is a single episode that illustrates why we must reform our monetary system, it is the failure of Quantitative Easing. Beginning in 2009 and ending in October of 2014, this unprecedented monetary expansion was supposed to revive the economy in the aftermath of the financial meltdown that the Fed's weak dollar policies helped create. The Fed added some $3.5 trillion to its balance sheet through bond purchases. The growth in bank reserves was proportionately twice what occurred in the 1970s. This was about equal to the size of the German economy.

Yet instead of reviving the economy, Quantitative Easing, the biggest peacetime expansion of bank reserves in U.S. history, produced the weakest-ever recovery from a major downturn. As we explain in the next chapter, Quantitative Easing and the suppression of interest rates hurt the flow of credit to small and new businesses that are the big job creators and ended up creating a *shortage* of dollars.

Finally, another problem with being dependent on government-manipulated money is that it permits countries to avoid tackling needed structural reforms, such as liberalizing markets. Instead, nations seeking to spur growth turn again and again to more government "stimulus" instead of instituting more effective measures like low taxes and sensible regulations.

In a world of sound money, it would be much harder to resort to such artificial activity. We would have far fewer bubbles and seismic disruptions. We can get things right on taxation, health-care, government spending, and regulation. But there is no hope for a true American renewal and a return to global sanity if we don't get money right.

CHAPTER 10

What's Wrong with the Federal Reserve and Why It Can't Guide the Economy

I F MONEY IS A MEASURE OF VALUE THAT SHOULD REMAIN CON-
stant, then what is to be done about the Federal Reserve? Its
Soviet-style control over the value and supply of money and
interest rates violates fundamental monetary principles. With its
far-reaching powers, today's Fed represents a break from America's
free-market tradition. Fed shenanigans have given us decades of
market bubbles and systemic crises—including the 2008 financial meltdown, produced by years of weakening the dollar. Yet
the Fed's countless policy missteps have for the most part skirted
widespread criticism.

The Fed and its "wise men" (and women) are treated with
hushed awe by politicians and the media because of the mystique
surrounding the subject of monetary policy. After the financial
crisis, our central bank was lauded for supposedly "rescuing" the
economy and "saving" the financial system, despite the role of its
weak dollar policies in that disaster. The blame fell on Wall Street,
"greedy" bankers, alleged bank deregulation, obtuse if not corrupt
credit rating agencies, and feckless politicians. Fed Chairman Ben

119

Bernanke was named "Person of the Year" by *Time*. And, to top it off, the central bank gained *increased* powers.

Thanks to the Dodd-Frank bill, the Fed holds regulatory sway over the U.S. banking system on a scale never seen before. It also has grown into the pre-eminent regulator, whose reach extends throughout the financial sector.

If we are to achieve meaningful change and a vigorous American Revival we must pull back the curtain and see the Fed for what it is: a central planning bureaucracy whose unbridled authority over credit and money is undermining America's entrepreneurial economy.

Created by an act of Congress in 1913, the Federal Reserve is comprised of twelve regional banks around the country. A governing body, the Federal Reserve Board, is centered in Washington. The Fed holds banks' reserves and provides financial services, such as clearing checks. It handles the banking needs of the U.S. government, exercises "regulatory and supervisory" powers over commercial banks, and—last but by no means least—determines monetary policy. This means trying to control the course of the economy by setting interest rates, primarily through "open market operations"—the buying or selling of Treasury securities (and occasionally other assets such as mortgage-backed securities) to increase or reduce the monetary base.

The Board Chair is a presidential appointee with a term of four years. The current Chair, Janet Yellen, assumed her post in 2014, succeeding Ben Bernanke, probably the worst Fed Chairman in history, responsible for three disastrous blunders that have done immense harm to the U.S.: weakening the dollar, Quantitative Easing, and zero interest rates.

Absent a world war, the Fed has never attempted to manipulate bond market interest rates as it did with its various iterations of Quantitative Easing. Almost every month until late 2014, our central bank bought billions of dollars of long-term U.S. government bonds and bundles of mortgages. The biggest peacetime monetary expansion in our history, QE was intended to "stimulate" the economy after the economic crisis of 2008–09. Instead, it helped produce the weakest-ever rebound from a major downturn, with annual growth rates stuck at around 2%.

The Fed's zero interest rates, also seen as a "stimulus," are another reason for the feeble recovery. That's because zero interest rates are, in effect, price controls. Interest is the price that lenders charge borrowers. The effect of price controls on any market, as anyone who has ever lived in a socialist or communist country will tell you, is shortages and rationing. With money it's no different.

Since 2009, the Fed by means of QE has amassed a portfolio of bonds and mortgages exceeding $3 trillion with money created out of thin air. But the low-interest loans made under this program went primarily to large corporations and to the government itself. Why? Because of the unusual and ultimately counterproductive bond-buying strategy the Fed used to push down interest rates known as *Operation Twist*.

Normally, the central bank expands the monetary base by buying short-term Treasuries from financial institutions. These purchases allow banks to make loans to the businesses that drive the American economy. In contrast, Operation Twist focused on lowering *long-term* interest rates by selling short-term Treasuries and buying long-term government bonds and mortgage-backed securities.

By artificially suppressing long-term interest rates, Operation Twist and QE were supposed to stimulate the economy by encouraging people to buy homes and businesses to invest. What really happened was that credit flowed to the politically favored. QE and Operation Twist facilitated the federal government's binge borrowing under Barack Obama. Uncle Sam's net cost of all of its new debt was virtually zero.

Meanwhile, large corporations borrowed more than they would have in a normal market because money was so cheap.

Apple, which has a staggering cash hoard of $200 billion, has issued some $40 billion of bonds. In part, this was to engage in financial engineering: for a while, the dividend yield on Apple's stock was *higher* than the interest rate it paid for 10-year bonds. So it sold the bonds and bought its own stock. Other major companies engaged in similar types of financial engineering to boost stock prices or reduce their tax burdens.

These corporations were only responding to opportunities created by a Fed-distorted market. Meanwhile, new and smaller companies that are the principal job creators had a harder time getting bank loans.

Also benefiting from Quantitative Easing were government-sponsored mortgage giants Fannie Mae and Freddie Mac. The two enterprises helped fuel the affordable housing mania that led to the financial crisis by pumping hundreds of billions of dollars into mortgages. Both entities ended up in government receivership. The Fed indirectly helped to revive them, thanks to fees they received from the sale of mortgage-backed securities.

Contrary to what supporters claim, the Fed is subject to the political winds in Washington. The result can be contradictory policy-making. For example: at the same time the Fed was implementing its massive stimulus, it was paying interest on bank reserves to prevent inflation. This discouraged banks from making loans to the job-creating businesses that would have spurred growth and recovery. Most of the QE liquidity never made it into the economy. It remained, and still remains, dammed up as bank reserves. What the Fed effectively did was to suck up an enormous portion of banks' lendable cash.

Credit markets are still not operating properly. The Fed's massive purchases of long-term Treasury bonds have created a shortage for insurers and pension funds that have long relied on these super-safe investments to help pay their policyholders and pensioners. Rock-bottom interest rates, meanwhile, have further squeezed their returns from these investments. Also hurt have been individual savers, especially the elderly, who have found themselves forced to take on riskier investments at a time when they can least afford to, because they get next to nothing on their bank certificates of deposit.

In the past five years, credit to small businesses and households grew only by 6% while credit to government expanded 37% and to corporations by 32%. Astute economist David Malpass draws the damning but inescapable conclusion: "The result was a dramatic swing toward big, established entities and away from growth. Small-business formation, critical for new jobs, has slowed accordingly. Wealth [is becoming] concentrated, because the artificially low rates benefit those who already have capital and assets at the expense of those who don't."

To this day, it is still difficult for entrepreneurial businesses to get loans and for many people to get a mortgage. Among them was noted economist Steve Moore, who wrote in frustration of being turned down for a mortgage, "Here we are with the lowest interest rates in 50 years, but many businesses and aspiring homeowners can't qualify. Water, water everywhere and not a drop to drink." But it gets worse:

> [H]ere is why I really want to pull my hair out. While I'm making a 25 percent down payment, the government insurance underwriters—the Federal Housing Administration (FHA), Fannie Mae and Freddie Mac—are backing with taxpayer dollars hundreds of thousands of low down payment loans of as little as 3 percent. These are the loans that will likely default. And taxpayers are on the hook for hundreds of billions of more loans. Uncle Sam is repeating every mistake it made just eight years ago.

The Fed's destructive and often contradictory policies ema-
nate from the Keynesian belief that manipulating the value of
money and rigging interest rates can create wealth and prosperity.
Congress itself mandated in the 1970s that the central bank work
to preserve "full employment," which the Fed has interpreted to
mean it must "stimulate" an ailing economy by weakening the currency. Federal Reserve Board Chair Janet Yellen's stated desire to
generate an inflation rate of 2%—a goal shared by countless other
central bank officials—reflects a long-discredited theory called the
Phillips curve. Disproven by seven Nobel Prize–winning economists and numerous others, the Phillips curve posits an ironclad
relationship between inflation and unemployment. If you want
low unemployment, you must generate inflation.

This is simply untrue. Economic historian Brian Domitrovic
has pointed out on Forbes.com that, in the inflationary boom/bust
era of the 1970s and early 1980s, unemployment reached higher
levels than during the financial crisis. In the 1980s, after Ronald
Reagan cut taxes and stabilized the dollar, in Domitrovic's words,
"inflation and unemployment both rappelled down a cliff."

The booming 1990s, moreover, was an era of low unemployment and declining inflation rates. Germany and Japan after World
War II similarly demonstrated that low inflation can go hand-in-
hand with soaring growth.

The idea that debasing the dollar is a good thing is the opposite of a reality Washington is intent on denying: that 2% inflation
rate is effectively a 2% tax hike, an increase in the cost of living.
How is that supposed to constructively stimulate the economy?

The answer is, of course, that it doesn't. But there is another question that should also be asked: If 2% inflation was the Fed's stated
goal, why have prices risen so *little*? The answer is that the Fed's
misguided QE allocating of credit, combined with the economy-
dampening effects of Dodd-Frank controls on the financial sector,
caused a shortage of dollars that has for now restrained inflation.

The Keynesian Fallacy and Its Impact

All of this gets to a central point: for all their air of seriousness and "wisdom," Fed bureaucrats can't "control" an economy. Their policies rarely hit their targets and instead end up causing damaging unintended consequences—like market bubbles. The Fed is based on a Keynesian premise of bureaucratic omnipotence that is utterly and completely false.

The idea that it's possible to use money to calibrate economic activity—as though the economy were a well-oiled machine—derives from the mistaken yet widely held notion that the economy is a self-contained entity capable of achieving "equilibrium." This fallacious belief is shared not only by Keynesians but also by Marxists, monetarists, classical economists, and even some supply-siders. Equilibrium supposedly is the economy's ideal resting state where all works as it should. In this nirvana, there should be "full employment," however one defines that. Supply should match demand. Prices should be stable.

If the economy were such a predictable entity, the Fed's forecasters would be far better than they are. At the beginning of every year since 2008, Fed economists have predicted its actions would produce a robust expansion, and each year it has had to sharply downgrade those expectations.

In his book, *Knowledge and Power,* George Gilder, the brilliant technologist and economist, points out that the presumption of forecasting is by nature a fallacy: "We cannot predict the value of our homes or prices on the stock market from day to day. We cannot anticipate illness or automobile accidents, the behavior of our children or the incomes of our parents. We cannot know the weather beyond a week or so. We cannot predict what course of college study will yield the best lifetime earnings or career. We are constantly startled by the news. We are almost entirely incapable of predicting the future."

What Keynesians fail to perceive is that the economy is not a mechanistic entity, but, as economist Joseph Schumpeter and others have observed, a dynamic, ever-evolving ecosystem with billions of people engaged in an incomprehensibly complex array of activities and transactions. In this turbulent environment, growth doesn't come from manipulating money but from revolutionary products and technologies like the smartphone or the Internet that improve living standards and create jobs.

Such innovations are inherently unpredictable, which is why Keynesian forecasts are so frequently wrong and why their monetary policies don't work. If the economy were a machine, it would resemble a Rube Goldberg contraption, where a single event sets off a succession of unintended consequences.

The most glaring example: Quantitative Easing, which was supposed to stimulate rapid economic growth. To the continuing surprise of the Fed, it has done the opposite. Instead of spurring the economy, the Fed inadvertently created an artificial shortage of dollars that sent commodity prices plunging. The economies of major commodity-producing countries such as Brazil, South Africa, Indonesia, and Russia have been sent into a tailspin.

Such events are compelling reasons why the Fed should not be in the business of attempting to micromanage the global economy by manipulating money. But this reality has been lost on the Keynesian-dominated political establishment. Thus, Washington's response to the financial crisis has been to give the Federal Reserve more power. Since 2008, the Federal Reserve has vastly increased its authority beyond that of a typical central bank. And it has done so with no real oversight or accountability. The former lender of last resort now has the much broader mission of preventing another crisis by maintaining the "financial stability" of the market. In addition to being a supreme act of hubris, the idea that any bureaucracy can ensure stable markets is as realistic as saying that man can control the weather.

More New Bureaucracies Are Crushing the Financial System's Efficiency and Effectiveness While Restricting Capital Flows

The Fed is imposing new layers of restrictions on lending in accordance with Basel III, high-toned regulatory standards devised by an international group of banking regulators known as the Basel Committee. Major U.S. banks have been required to substantially increase capital or decrease their lending activities. Regulators now minutely examine almost every loan to make sure it is not "too risky." Banks must require more collateral and impose other restrictions that they would not have imposed before the financial crisis. This has heaped crushing costs on smaller banks. Basel has put a dampener on normal bank lending to small and new businesses. Bank examiners take a wary view of anything that could be construed as "risky."

The Fed dominates a new entity called the Financial Stability Board (FSB), which includes the Treasury Secretary and the heads of various regulatory agencies. This board has labeled certain financial firms "Systemically Important Financial Institutions" (SIFI). Financial institutions unlucky enough to be branded an SIFI are shackled with still more regulations. The board is applying this designation not only to banks but also to insurance companies. The FSB also wants to use the SIFI label to sink its claws into major mutual fund companies, hedge and equity funds, and venture capital firms as well.

This has dire implications for the capital markets that have long been the lifeblood of the American economy. Life insurance companies, for example, have traditionally been important sources of capital for American businesses. SIFI-labeled institutions get hit with regulations diverting crucial resources, making them less able to fulfill this critical role. One insurer, MetLife, is courageously fighting its SIFI designation in the courts and appears to have a good chance of victory.

Then there's another new Fed bureaucracy established by Dodd-Frank legislation: the extraordinarily powerful Consumer Financial Protection Bureau (CFPB), intended to "protect" people from evil practices of banks and consumer lenders. This unelected agency does not answer to Congress and is funded by the Fed, no questions asked. Accountable to no one, it is running amuck, using its power over the financial industry to further various political agendas. The CFPB is waging a jihad against auto dealers, trying to force banks to deny financing to those allegedly not providing enough credit to minority customers. Congressional requests to agency bureaucrats to provide *evidence* that car sellers are practicing racial discrimination went ignored. The reason: there wasn't any.

Another CFPB overreach: demanding the monthly card statements of almost every American to see if it can ferret out possible abuses on the part of credit card companies. What abuses? They don't know. This exercise is a pure fishing expedition by an agency trying to justify its existence.

Privacy advocates were outraged when the National Security Agency (NSA) scooped up phone records of millions of Americans to identify suspicious calling patterns in the name of national security. But there was relatively little outcry over the CFPB invasion of privacy, which involves collecting far more information. The agency promised it would not abuse personal credit card records and that they would be secure. All we have to do is look at the record of other government agencies—like the IRS—to see how well such promises are usually kept.

So, What Can We Do?

Our answer: The Federal Reserve System should be sharply down-sized. Its bank regulatory functions should be transferred to a new agency and its research functions privatized.

In addition to handling the banking chores of the U.S. government, the Fed should have only two tasks: The first should be keeping the dollar stable in value, which would be best achieved by reverting to the gold standard. The second should be dealing decisively and quickly with the occasional panic. The Bank of England demonstrated how this should be done back in the 1860s. Banks would put up collateral for short-term loans from the Fed, preferably at above market interest rates. As the emergency subsides, the loans are rapidly repaid.

In advance of those big reforms, some constructive measures can be taken right now to restore some sanity to the system.

- *Let the costs of borrowing and lending money begin to reflect true market conditions:* More lending will result as price controls and distortions are removed.
- *Shrink the Fed's obese portfolio as bonds and mortgages mature:* This would remove QE and Operation Twist's credit distortions and stimulate more lending, thereby invigorating our sluggish economy.
- *Cease the hyperregulation of banks:* This means, among other things, stopping the ridiculous stress tests that have the effect of inhibiting lending to small borrowers. Let banks live with the consequences—good and bad—of their own decisions.
- *Declare the Basel Accords null and void:* Or at least simply ignore them. They have pushed banks to make unsound decisions on lending and on purchasing securities. For instance, under Basel, government bonds are considered far

less risky than loans to businesses. Until Greece's financial crisis went public, its bonds were considered a sounder use of bank money than a loan to a company like IBM. We don't need Basel to make sensible judgments regarding adequate levels of capital. Bankers should be left to make their own decisions. If they make too many bad ones, their institutions should be liquidated or broken up.

- *Cease applying the SIFI label* to any entity that engages in financial activities.

- *End the growing politicization of regulation:* One example: BB&T is one of the nation's largest banks. It is also the best-capitalized big bank. Yet a couple of years ago, the Fed declared that it had flunked its stress test. The real reason for this failure: bank management was too open in criticizing Washington's boneheaded decisions during and after the crisis of 2008–09. This also means revenue-hungry politicians must desist from treating banks as their own piggy banks. Government agencies on both the state and federal level have gotten into the nasty habit of conjuring up alleged bank wrongdoing as a means of extracting multi-billion dollar settlements from them. Banks, well aware of their political unpopularity and how their well-being depends these days on regulatory sufferance, go along. And no more "suggesting" to banks that they cut off politically incorrect clients such as gun dealers.

The Fed was founded after the Panic of 1907 to provide an emergency source of cash to banks in the event of a crisis or to meet seasonal surges in demand from the large agricultural sector (farm laborers were paid in the fall after the harvest). Its core mission was also to keep the dollar on the gold standard. Obviously, it has wandered far afield. The U.S. needs a central bank. But if the economy is to regain its footing, the Fed must be scaled back from the overreaching behemoth it is today to the institution that its founders intended.

CHAPTER 11

The Best Way to Stable Money Is the Gold Standard

WHY IS PEGGING THE DOLLAR TO GOLD THE FOUNDA-tion of our monetary reforms? The answer is simple: it is the best way to achieve truly sound and stable money.

Gold is not perfect. But it maintains its value better than anything else on earth. It is to commerce and money what Polaris, the North Star, is to navigation: a constant.

Gold has unique features. It is rare but not too rare. Gold cannot be destroyed. Every ounce extracted from the earth is still in existence. Experts estimate that, worldwide, some 6 billion ounces have been mined and around 5-and-a-half billion are accounted for today. Roy Jastram observed in his classic work *The Golden Constant*, "The ring worn today may contain particles mined in the time of the pharaohs."

Unlike commodities like wheat or corn that are vulnerable to weather conditions, gold is not subject to supply shocks that can drastically affect its price. Nor do you consume it as you would oranges or oil. What if there's a major find, as has happened several times in history? The huge inflows of gold and silver from Spain's American colonies produced price increases averaging under 2%

133

a year. The California Gold Rush of 1849, the biggest discovery ever, vastly increased the average annual production of gold but the resulting inflation was minimal and quickly receded. With the enormous South African discoveries of the 1890s, along with big finds in Alaska and Australia, there was a surge in the world supply. But the increase in gold also had a small impact on prices just like the California Gold Rush.

Some may wonder: Why not silver? Like gold, it has been used as money. But its intrinsic value and supply are less stable. Governments have tried every alternative to a gold standard, including what we have today—no standard at all. But whenever gold is abandoned, it inevitably reemerges for the simple reason that nothing has worked better.

The reason: Linking the dollar to gold is the best way to sound money. The value of a dollar would be as certain as the number of inches in a foot or the number of minutes in an hour. The impact on the American and world economies would be huge. America would experience an historic resurgence that would potentially exceed the explosion of wealth creation that took place in the late 19th century during the era of the classical gold standard.

We don't hear much these days about that period in world history. Those skeptical of gold don't realize that, in the late 19th century, most nations of the world *spontaneously* adopted a gold standard. They were inspired by the example of Britain, which had become a global economic and political power after the head of the mint, Sir Isaac Newton, tied the pound to gold in 1717 at the rate of 3.89 pounds per ounce, a ratio that lasted more than two centuries.

Fixing the pound to gold meant that Britain's lenders would be paid back in money that wouldn't lose its value. The resulting increase in investor confidence produced an explosion in capital creation. Sound money helped create capital markets that turned

Britain from a second-tier island nation into the mightiest industrial power in the world. Britain's robust financial sector helped finance the steam engine, railroads, and countless other advances of the Industrial Revolution. The city of Manchester became a center of manufacturing and innovation—the era's equivalent of Silicon Valley.

The United States had a similar experience after instituting a gold standard during the presidency of George Washington. The young nation had previously endured the horrors of fiat money in the form of hyperinflation during the War of Independence. Alexander Hamilton, the first Secretary of the Treasury, was inspired by the success of Britain's economy, which was largely founded on its modern financial system created by the Bank of England and the gold standard. Hamilton put in a new and stable tax system. He fixed the dollar by law to a specific weight of gold—$19.39 per ounce. (There was a slight devaluation in 1834 to $20.67 an ounce.)

The transformation was swift: overseas capital poured in, including from our onetime adversary Great Britain. The United States rapidly emerged as a major economic power, surpassing even England by the end of the 19th century. This economic miracle took place despite a U.S. banking system weighed down by countless restrictions and regulations.

Other countries soon sought to emulate the monetary system responsible for the successes of America and Britain. Germany, Italy, Spain, France, Russia, Japan, and even Greece all adopted gold-based money. The global economy experienced an unequaled explosion in trade, capital creation, and investment for the following 100 years.

The late 19th century was literally a golden era. The gold standard worked because leaders and governments, unlike those of our era, understood the importance of sound money.

In more recent times, stable money helped both Germany and Japan recover from the devastation of World War II. After the war, Germany's money supply was five times the level it had been in the late 1930s. Germany's economy was plagued by inflation and shortages. Things got so bad that by one estimate as many as half of all transactions were taking place through barter. Ludwig Erhard, Germany's newly appointed director of the Office of Economic Opportunity, replaced the overabundant and near worthless Reichsmark with the Deutschmark pegged to the gold-based U.S. dollar. In addition, he decontrolled prices, stopped all rationing (which appalled the Allied occupiers), and began slashing taxes. With its open markets and stable currency, Germany snapped back and quickly became Europe's foremost economic power. Erhard subsequently became economics minister of the newly formed Federal Republic of Germany and later its Chancellor.

A similar series of events occurred in post-war Japan. American occupation authorities appointed banker Joseph Dodge to address Japan's virulent inflation. In 1949, he instituted the Dodge plan, which stabilized Japan's currency, pegging the yen to the gold-based dollar. The new financial system, along with frequent tax cuts, enabled Japan to achieve growth rates comparable to those of present-day China. Japan became one of the premier world economies, eventually surpassing Germany in size.

If the United States adopted a gold standard, we would see an explosion of economic growth far in excess of the paltry results of Quantitative Easing. By encouraging investment, a gold standard would produce a more powerful economic stimulus than anything Fed bureaucrats have been able to achieve.

There would be other benefits, too. A sound and stable dollar linked to gold would mean the end of the kind of commodity and housing bubbles we've seen in the past decade-and-a-half. It would also stop the long-term erosion of the value of the dollar that has taken place as a result of Fed-engineered inflation.

Gold would take the distortions out of the price system, enabling prices to convey genuine market values. In other words, gold would enable money, for the first time in decades, to properly fulfill its role as a communicator of value and facilitator of trade.

With a gold standard, a central bank would not have to artificially lower interest rates. They would come down automatically. Lenders would not need to charge such high rates because they'd be repaid in money that has not declined in value.

This is exactly what unfolded in the 19th-century gold standard era. "Interest rates worldwide converged to low levels," observes monetary historian Nathan Lewis. "British debt was perceived to have the lowest risk of either credit default or currency devaluation." The story was much the same in other countries where the gold standard reigned. Yields on French government debt, for example, were at a catastrophic 15% when the Bank of France was established in 1800. By 1902, the rate was a mere 3%.

We'd see the same effects today if we instituted a gold standard. While interest rates would be somewhat higher than they are now—after all, you can't get much lower than zero—the result would be a vigorous and well-functioning capital market. Credit would flow freely again. Lenders would have a market-based price on which to base their loans. The artificial scarcities created by the Fed's zero interest rate would cease to exist. Small and new businesses would no longer be starved for credit and capital.

With a gold-linked dollar there would also be no inflation. No inflation, however, does not mean that prices stay the same. Prices would continue to rise and fall. But their fluctuations would be in response to genuine changes in supply, demand, and productivity. In other words, prices would reflect *real values.*

Average housing prices, for example, might still go up. But they would not rise because of artificially cheap money flooding the mortgage market—but because of growing incomes and people desiring bigger abodes with more and fancier amenities.

Remember, it's easier to trade and invest when money is sound. If anyone doubts how unstable money inhibits commerce, one need only look to the example of a chronic inflator like Brazil and its dead-in-the-water economy.

There are other reasons to return to gold. Among them: gold takes the politics out of money. We think of the Fed as being above the political fray. But that's not true. In 1971, Arthur Burns, then Chairman of the Fed, went along with the plan to sever the dollar's link to gold to make it easier to weaken the greenback and deliver a temporary charge to the U.S. economy, thus helping Nixon win re-election. The excessively low interest rates in place since 2009 have also enabled the Obama administration to more easily finance its massive expansion of government.

Gold would make it harder for bureaucrats to engage in such political manipulation. It holds government accountable: No longer could politicians make easy promises and count on a printing press to pay for them. Raising more revenue requires that government borrow or impose higher taxes—transparent actions with political consequences. In the words of gold standard advocate Daniel Ryan:

> Government can still borrow, but they can't use the central bank to sidestep the consequences of excessive borrowing that every other borrower has to face: higher interest rates. A gold standard would forbid quantitative easing. Thus, a gold standard puts a lid on the shenanigans politicians like to use for political gain. We've all seen the effects of leaving monetary and fiscal discretion in the hands of politicians and their appointees: chronic inflation and chronic government debt. Had there been a gold standard, government debt would have never gotten out of hand like it has.

Big Government proponents fear that this kind of account-ability would mean government austerity. Not at all. The German welfare state developed under Otto Bismarck in the late 1800s when the country was bound by the classical gold standard. Great Britain, the originator of the gold standard, enacted a number of social welfare programs right up to the beginning of World War I.

We're not supporters of Big Government. But statists shouldn't fear gold. In fact, by boosting the economy, gold would grow the tax base and thus tax receipts. The cost of servicing government debt would be less over time because of gold's lower interest rates. That would make paying for government easier.

What gold does is take decisions about the value and supply of money out of the hands of politicians and bureaucrats who know a lot less then they'd like us to believe. We may be in awe of the Fed's "high priests." But they can no more guess the need for money than central planners could run an economy in the days of the Soviet Union. Seemingly sophisticated equations and various measures of money will never anticipate how people actually act. Despite their delusion, central bankers can't control the supply of money, which ultimately results from people buying and selling to each other. Money is similar to a claim check on products and services. In addition, central bankers can't control what is called *the velocity of money*, that is, how many times a dollar turns over.

No bureaucrat or central planner can anticipate the demand for money, which reflects the ever-shifting actions and desires of billions of people in global markets. Gold prices convey these changing needs better than anything else.

In a monetary system based on a gold standard, the role of the central bank would simply be to maintain a stable currency in terms of gold. The value of the dollar would be pegged to a par-ticular weight of gold, for example, $1,100 per ounce, or to put it another way, a dollar would equal 1/1100 an ounce of gold. If the price threatens to drop, that means there may not be enough liquidity in the economy. The central bank could engage in open-market operations or use other tools to increase liquidity. When the price of gold starts to rise that means that there may be too many dollars floating around and it's time to tighten up. Gold acts as a barometer of the amount of money the market needs.

A rise in the gold price indicates whether there's too much liquidity—too much money in the economy—and that we're heading toward inflation. A drop in its price indicates that there's too little liquidity and the possibility of deflation.

Maintaining a constant dollar value, therefore, doesn't mean a rigid money supply. Most gold skeptics, however, persist in this misguided focus on supply, which is a major barrier to an understanding of gold. Indeed, we explain in our next chapter that a nation can institute a gold standard without owning any gold at all.

CHAPTER 12

How a Gold Standard
Would Work

H OW WOULD A GOLD STANDARD WORK? THAT DEPENDS on which one we're talking about. Most people don't realize that there are several systems of gold-based money. The *classical gold standard* was the system established by Britain and eventually used during the late 1800s by the world's largest economies, until the outbreak of World War I. A second system, the *gold exchange standard*, was used after both world wars. Another two have been proposed: a *100% gold-backed currency* and what we call the *gold price system*. All have their critics and supporters, and the methodologies differ. But one feature is constant: gold is the yardstick of value. Below, a brief guide to the four gold standard systems.

The Classical Gold Standard

Nathan Lewis, one's of today's pre-eminent authorities on money, has called the classical gold standard, "The most perfect monetary system humans have yet created." Yet it remains to this day misunderstood. For instance, people who have seen too many movies mistakenly believe that commerce was conducted with gold coins during the era of the classical gold standard. Gold coins did exist and circulate. But in the latter part of the 1800s, people used paper notes as they do today. Under a classical gold standard system, countries pegged their currencies to a particular weight of gold. You could take your paper notes to the bank and exchange them for gold at a fixed rate, or you could swap gold for cash.

Another mistaken belief is that money under a classical gold standard is 100% backed by gold bullion stored in a bank vault. Gold bullion reserve coverage in the United States in 1901 was 42% of banknotes in circulation. This coverage ratio varied from country to country. But the end result was always stable money. The system worked!

During the classical gold standard era, governments possessed gold reserves in the form of gold bars. Most also had bonds denominated in foreign gold-based currencies. Convertibility, however, was sacrosanct. For example, if people feared the government was printing too much money, then they could exchange their money for gold.

To head off a drop in gold reserves, a government in those days would quiet fears by taking steps to demonstrate fiscal prudence. It might raise interest rates to attract money, increase taxes, or cut spending—anything to reassure markets that there would be no deficit to invite heedless money printing.

A major misunderstanding about the gold standard is that it requires a country to have its exports and imports roughly balance out. The thinking is that importing more than exporting is a sign of weakness, like a company losing money. This fails to take into account investment dollars that return to the economy. These "capital flows" can even exceed the dollars leaving as a result of trade. The United States with its rapidly growing economy ran chronic trade deficits and was an enormous importer of capital. Nonetheless, the dollar stayed fixed to gold except during the Civil War and its immediate aftermath.

What brought an end to the era of the classical gold standard, we've explained earlier, was World War I. The need to pay for war has always trumped the commitment to sound money. Throughout history, governments have sought to finance their armies by clipping coins or, in modern times, turning on the printing press. The pressures of a major war have always led to inflation.

The most practical response after the Great War would have been for countries to return to a gold standard with their money pegged to gold at ratios based on post-war values. Instead, statesmen became fixated on gold supplies. They were convinced there was not enough gold to provide adequate coverage for all the new money created. The British were particularly obsessed with the idea, but feared that setting a new gold ratio would cause people to lose faith in the pound. This woefully misguided analysis led Britain to return to its prewar gold price, resulting in labor strife, social turmoil, and a subpar economy.

The Gold Exchange Standard

The gold exchange standard was the system implemented after both World Wars when people feared—wrongly—that there wasn't enough gold to maintain a classical gold standard. A few countries also used it during the era of the classical gold standard.

Under a gold exchange standard, nations peg their monies to one, possibly two "target" or "reserve" currencies that are directly tied to gold, such as the dollar or the British pound. To keep their money linked to the target currency at a fixed exchange rate, they use traditional monetary tools, such as open market operations or intervening (e.g., buying or selling your nation's currency) in foreign exchange markets, to keep their money correctly pegged to the reserve currency.

With a gold exchange standard, the government could hold some gold, but the bulk of the reserves would be government bonds denominated in reserve currencies. Such bonds were considered a gold equivalent because they were denominated in currencies directly tied to gold. Countries loved this because bonds pay interest while gold does not. Their reserves, therefore, could grow. If a nation wanted the yellow metal, it could simply sell dollar- or pound-denominated bonds and turn the cash in for gold.

Gold standard purists, however, have long regarded this system as "gold standard lite." They see substituting bonds for gold as an invitation to inflation. Creating new bonds, after all, is a lot easier for governments than increasing reserves of the yellow metal. Such skeptics are convinced that the gold exchange standard created excessive credit that led to the stock market bubble and the crash of 1929. But as we explain in our chapter on the myths about gold, this notion is based on a misunderstanding of how the system works and a misreading of history.

For example, commodity prices would have jumped if there had been an inflationary amount of money in circulation. Instead, in the 1920s, commodity prices were either flat or declining. That's one reason why American farmers experienced distress despite the era's booming economy.

Both versions of the gold exchange standard collapsed, not because of inherent flaws, but because the guardians of the system—Britain after WWI and the U.S. after WWII—were unwilling to abide by its discipline. Britain in 1931 mistakenly devalued the pound to fight the Great Depression. The U.S. in 1971 did the same thing to combat a very mild recession.

The Gold Price System, or the "Dollar Bill" System

U.S. Representative Ted Poe of Texas several years ago introduced legislation to enact this modern version of the gold standard. Its great virtue is that, unlike past standards, a nation need not have a pile of gold for the system to function. Here's how it works: the dollar would be pegged to gold at, for instance, $1,100 an ounce. If the price of gold rose beyond that level, the Federal Reserve would move to bring it back to $1,100 by reducing the money supply. If the opposite occurred—i.e., the price dipped *below* $1,100—the Fed would expand the supply either by increasing bank reserves or encouraging banks to make more loans

Under this system, the Fed would no longer be allowed to set interest rates, except for interest it charged on loans to a bank during an emergency. Its role would be to increase or decrease the monetary base in order to maintain a fixed gold price.

In other words, under the gold price system *you don't need to own an ounce of gold.* Forbes.com contributor Louis Woodhill has noted that an advantage of this system is that it's not vulnerable to pressure from speculators buying up supplies.

How do you get the right gold/dollar ratio? After all, you don't want to set the price of gold too low and end up with the kind of deflation that ensued when Great Britain made this mistake after World War I. The soundest approach would be to set a price based on a 10-year or even 5-year average of the gold/dollar price, marked up 10% as insurance against deflation.

What About a 100% Gold-Backed System?

We need to answer this question because some gold standard supporters advocate such a system. They distrust even a classical gold standard, where only a portion of the money supply is covered by gold. They equate partial coverage with our modern system of "fractional reserve banking," whereby banks lend out most of their depositors' money, keeping only a fraction on hand as reserves. They consider both systems dangerously dependent on leverage and inherently unstable.

Thus, they believe that any gold standard should require a government to possess enough gold to support a country's entire money stock—enough to redeem 100% of depositors' money. This would supposedly eliminate the risk of bank failures. Advocates also claim that, since the global gold supply grows at about 2% a year, in line with long-term economic growth rates, a 100% system would not be deflationary.

They're wrong. A 100% gold-backed system would result in either a terrible inflation or a horrific deflation. Why? The current U.S. monetary base is over $4 trillion. Before Quantitative Easing, it was a little under $900 billion. The U.S. today holds 261 million ounces of gold, which at today's market price comes to almost $300 billion. To achieve 100% gold backing would therefore mean a gargantuan contraction of the money supply. This would destroy the economy.

The other way to achieve 100% coverage would be to increase the price of gold. Franklin Roosevelt did that in 1934 when he jacked up the dollar price of gold from $20.67 to $35. But that is small change compared to what these advocates are proposing. To get 100% gold backing this way would mean the gold/dollar price would have to balloon from about $1,100 to almost $15,000 an ounce. That would give us the kind of inflation that destroyed Germany after World War I, leading to the rise of Adolf Hitler.

Some supporters of 100% backing want such a system to be administered by a currency board in place of the Fed. Usually under a currency board, a nation's money is backed 100% by the currency of another country.

Unlike a central bank, a currency board has no discretion. It holds a particular currency, perhaps supplemented with bonds in that currency. But it does not borrow or lend. The sole focus of a currency board is maintaining an unchanging exchange rate with the currency of another nation that is seen as more stable. Countries like Bulgaria will use these mechanistic entities to fix their currencies to the euro or the dollar.

Currency boards have been around for over 150 years. You don't need a gold-based system to operate one. In addition to

Bulgaria, Denmark, Lithuania, and a number of African states use them today. These currency boards all use the euro. Hong Kong has had a dollar-based currency board since 1983.

Johns Hopkins economics professor Steve Hanke, an expert who has helped design currency boards for a number of nations, has suggested that a currency board in a gold-based system could "hold reserves in gold or in highly rated or liquid securities either denominated in gold or fully hedged against changes in the fiat-currency price of gold."

Could such an entity work with a 100% gold-backed system? Perhaps in a small country, but not in the United States. As we explain above, there's simply not enough gold to do it.

Bottom line: a gold standard based on 100% coverage is simply not feasible—which is why no such system has ever existed.

Which Is It? Our Proposal for a 21st Century Hybrid

Are we advocating a return to the classical gold standard, a gold exchange standard—or the gold price system?

Our answer is a system that incorporates the best aspects of each.

Obviously, gold is the yardstick of value. However, a 21st century gold standard would not require holding stockpiles of gold. There would be no need to manipulate interest rates or fret about whether we have a trade surplus or deficit. The key is the willingness—and the knowledge—to defend and maintain the ratio between gold and the dollar. Let's look at the basic features of our proposed reformed system.

The Dollar Will Have a Fixed Value That the Fed Must Maintain by Law

As with previous gold standards, the 21st-century system would have a set gold/dollar ratio. That price could be determined primarily using a 5- or 10-year average of gold prices with a mark-up to help prevent a deflation. The Federal Reserve would be required by law to maintain this value through open market operations, the setting of bank reserves, and/or the direct purchase or sale of gold.

Transition to the New System Would Be Gradual

The new standard could be up and running within a year. The government would announce in advance a specific date for the change to take place. This would allow markets to adjust to the prospect of a stable, gold-based dollar. With no more fears of weak or strong money, you would see the true intrinsic price of gold emerge. This natural market price would help determine the eventual gold-to-dollar ratio. Investors would quickly adjust to the new environment. However, financial institutions, especially banks, would experience a more wrenching change because their huge currency trading operations would be scaled back dramatically. With the dollar stable, most other countries would quickly fix their currencies to the greenback. The violent fluctuations of recent decades would be history.

For operational purposes, the dollar would be permitted to go up or down against gold within a range of 1%.

The 21st Century Gold Standard Would Be Instituted Through an Act of Congress

That way the Federal Reserve could no longer exercise the "discretion" that has given us disastrous policies like Quantitative Easing. The principle goal of the Fed would be to maintain the gold/dollar ratio. The new law would also bar the Fed from manipulating interest rates, whether short-term or long-term. The one exception would be the interest rate that banks pay to borrow money from the Fed, preferably above existing market rates. This would prevent banks from using the Fed as a cheap source of money.

No More Barriers to Alternative Currencies Like Bitcoin

This feature would act as a safeguard against Washington—as it has in the past—violating the gold standard, even one required by law. After all, we've seen presidents take action without legal authority. The ability to create alternative currencies, including crypto-currencies like Bitcoin, would enable people to protect themselves and their wealth from government mischief. A move to such currencies would be a powerful signal that Americans are losing faith in the soundness of their currency. It would tell us that the government's monetary policy is going off the tracks and must be corrected. To date, investing in alternative currencies is discouraged by various taxes and fees on the sale of gold and silver, as well as by capital gains taxes. These levies, in addition to burdensome reporting rules on major gold and silver buyers, should be eliminated.

Another Safeguard: Allow Conversion of Dollars Into Gold

A 21st century gold standard would restore the right of Americans to convert dollars into gold at a fixed rate. While not necessary for a modern gold standard, convertibility provides one more safeguard against misbehavior by the Federal Reserve. If the Fed is not doing its job, people could take direct action, as they could under the classic gold standard. There would be no need for a formal gold cover. Instead, the U.S. government would be required to keep, say, around 50 million ounces of gold on hand. (Its total supply is 261 million ounces today.) If there was a run on gold—which would only occur if the Fed is violating the standard—the U.S. would be obliged to buy more yellow metal to make sure the reserves didn't fall below the 50 million threshold. This would discourage misbehavior by the Fed and keep the dollar price stable. Meanwhile, Washington's gold holdings, and the Fed itself, would be audited annually.

Finally, we would encourage that dollar-to-gold transactions take place through private dealers by requiring that Uncle Sam charge a hefty premium for the buying or selling of gold. We don't want a Fannie Mae equivalent in the gold markets.

Other Countries Would Link Their Money to the Dollar

Numerous nations already do this informally because it makes trading and investing in the U.S. easier. We discuss in the following chapter the importance of understanding how to maintain such a link. A country like China and the European nations that rely on the euro might wish to have their own gold-based system. That would be fine. The competition to see who had the best currency would be beneficial for all.

As for the Fed . . .

The central bank would return to its original role as lender of last resort, a source of emergency liquidity for the system in the event of a trauma like the unexpected collapse of a major financial institution. The Fed would also continue to provide banking services for government and commercial banks, as it does now. But a gold standard would take away the Fed's control over credit and money. The institution would be shorn of its immense powers—and the ability to wreak havoc in the economy.

CHAPTER 13

Debunking
the Gold Myths

I F THE GOLD STANDARD IS THE WAY TO BRING BACK A TRULY
healthy American economy, then why hasn't the United States
already returned to it? Because Keynesians and monetarists
have long dominated the policymaking establishment. Like the
European mercantilists who equated a nation's wealth with its
stores of bullion, today's economists believe that increasing the
supply of money stimulates an economy. They dismiss the need
for a sound, gold-based currency. This misunderstanding crosses
political boundaries. President Ronald Reagan was a believer in
sound money. He recognized that, in the words of John F. Kennedy,
a nation should have a sound currency and that the dollar should
be "as good as gold." He created a Gold Commission in 1981
whose purpose was to examine the future role of gold in our monetary system. But because of the vagaries of Washington politics,
its membership ended up stacked with anti-gold fanatics. With the
exception of the brilliant economist Arthur Laffer (known for the
Laffer curve), Reagan's advisors were predominantly monetarists
unanimously opposed to gold. This opposition kiboshed any hope
of a new gold-based Bretton Woods-like system. However, if only
Reagan had his way, we would have a gold standard today.

151

Then as now, the overwhelming influence of Keynesians and monetarists limited criticism of fiat money and allowed myths and misconceptions about the gold standard to go largely unchallenged. Below we list the most common arguments against gold and show that the argument quickly falls apart in the face of reality.

Myth: *Gold is not a reliable anchor because its price fluctuates dramatically.*

Reality: *The price of gold reflects marketplace perceptions of the value of paper currencies.*

Opponents insist that gold's fluctuating price means that a gold-based dollar would produce roller coaster prices throughout the economy. Economist Barry Eichengreen typifies this thinking when he writes that "gold's inherent price volatility" makes it unable to "provide a basis for international commercial and financial transactions on a twenty-first century scale."

Liberal columnist Ezra Klein insists that, "The problems with the gold standard are legion but the most obvious is that our currency fluctuates with the global price of gold as opposed to the needs of our economy."

This gets it backwards. A hard asset, gold has traditionally been an investment haven when people have some reason to distrust the value of their currency—when they see it being debased. We explained earlier that during such times money tends to flow into not just gold but also oil and other commodities, as well as hard assets like housing and land. A good part of gold's price reflects anticipated inflation and uncertainty about the future.

For instance, in 2010, the price of gold shot up thanks to anxieties over the Fed-created weakening of the dollar that started in the early 2000s. There were also fears that Quantitative Easing—the biggest peacetime monetary expansion of bank reserves in recent history—would lead to hyperinflation. In 2011, gold shot to a record high of $1,900. The spike was fueled by additional fears that the U.S. government might default on its bonds because of a fight between the Obama administration and congressional Republicans over raising the government debt ceiling.

Since then such apprehensions have quieted and gold has responded accordingly, retreating to around $1,100 an ounce in late 2015. Other commodity prices have similarly fallen, though they are still far above what they were in the pre-crisis 1990s, before the millennial weakening of the dollar.

A similar scenario played out in 1980 when observers worried that the United States would be incapable of controlling ever-worsening inflation: the dollar price of gold shot from $220 in 1979 to $850 an ounce. Then a new administration took office. Paul Volcker, Ronald Reagan's Fed Chairman, set about taming the inflation that had characterized the Carter era, by tightening up on the dollar. Emotions calmed, the dollar price fell to $300 an ounce.

Gold prices fluctuated between $325 and $440 an ounce through the Reagan era and into the 1990s, a period known as the Great Moderation, an era of minimal Fed monkey business.

Myth: *There is not enough gold in today's world for governments to use a gold standard.*
Reality: *A gold standard is about value, not supply. Governments can have a working gold standard without owning an ounce of gold.*

The United States has only about 261 million ounces of gold with a market price of roughly $284 billion. The monetary base is over $4 trillion, and the most commonly used money supply measure, M2, is now over $12 trillion. Gold critics insist that, with such vastly expanded money supplies, not just in the U.S. but worldwide, there is no longer enough precious metal to permit governments to maintain a gold standard that would support today's prices.

If the dollar were pegged to gold at its current value, they say, we would have to undergo a searing deflation. What they don't recognize is that what makes gold work is not its supply, but rather its ability to act as a yardstick of value. For gold to work effectively as a measure, governments don't need to possess piles of this precious metal any more than a builder needs warehouses of tape measures to construct a hotel or a bridge.

Even during the era of the classical gold standard, no country ever had 100% gold backing for its money. The ratio in the U.S. was around 42% in the early 1900s and had been lower before then. Great Britain also had very low amounts of gold backing the pound, but no one minded because the Bank of England knew how to manage the system. Coverage ratios varied from country to country.

A 21st-century gold standard would easily work with our current supply. Even if the United States decided to give people the legal right to redeem dollars for gold, the U.S. would still have enough of the metal to make such a system work.

Myth: *A gold standard would result in a rigid supply of money inhibiting economic growth.*
Reality: *Under a gold standard, the money supply would fluctuate naturally based on the needs of the economy.*

Gold skeptics like former Fed Chairman Ben Bernanke fear that a fixed gold price would prevent growth in the money supply, making money overly expensive and restraining economic growth. Bernanke expressed this concern in a college lecture, where he worried that, "Because the money supply is determined by the supply of gold, it cannot be adjusted in response to changing economic conditions."

Advocates of ever-bigger government similarly fear that gold means a rigid money supply that would restrain government from printing more money to pay for social welfare programs.

Larry White explains that Bernanke's warning is a fallacy because, "[U]nder a gold standard, a change in the money supply can also be brought about by market forces. Under a gold standard, market forces in gold mining, minting, and banking *do* adjust the money supply in response to changing economic conditions, that is, in response to changes in the demand to hold monetary gold or to hold bank-issued money."

The critics again miss the point: a gold standard does not mean having a fixed supply of money but maintaining *a stable dollar value.*

Under a gold standard, keeping the dollar stable would mean that the supply of money *would have to fluctuate* in response to rising or falling economic activity. A lesson from history: the U.S. money supply *exploded* between 1775 and 1900, when the dollar was fixed to gold. America was transforming from an agrarian nation into an industrial society; its population expanded from about 3 million to 76 million. More people and commerce needed more money: the supply *multiplied by 160-fold.* A gold standard does not restrict the supply of dollars any more than a foot made up of 12 inches restricts the number of rulers being used in the economy.

What if we had another banking crisis like the panic of 2008, which called for an emergency injection of liquidity in order to keep the financial system from imploding? Gold would in no way prevent such an intervention. Banks could still obtain emergency loans from the Fed. It's worth noting that the model of "lender of last resort" was developed by the Bank of England in the 1860s, during the era of the classical gold standard.

The need for emergency loans under a gold standard, however, would be far less likely. As astute monetary expert Nathan Lewis has observed on Forbes.com, stable money has never caused a financial crisis.

Myth: *Gold caused the Great Depression.*
Reality: *The Great Depression was the result of a global trade war triggered by U.S. enactment of the Smoot–Hawley tariff.*

You'll also hear gold blamed for helping to bring on the Great Depression. According to this narrative, fear of creating a run on gold in Great Britain kept the U.S. from raising interest rates and curbing its overheating stock market in the roaring '20s. This, believers say, produced a credit bubble and a falsely inflated economy, culminating in the crash of 1929.

In fact, the Great Depression was a disastrous consequence of the global trade war ignited by America's enactment of the Smoot-Hawley Tariff Act in June of 1930. This toxic and totally unprecedented act of protectionism imposed an average 60% tax on over 3,000 import items. The stock market crashed in the fall of 1929 when it appeared that Smoot-Hawley would likely pass Congress. When the law's prospects subsequently appeared to dim, the market rebounded, ending the year roughly where it had begun. In 1930, when the legislation reemerged, the slide resumed.

America's trading partners responded to Smoot-Hawley's battery of tariffs with their own retaliatory measures. The resulting worldwide trade war delivered a blow to global commerce commensurate with the onset of World War I.

Policy makers—in the U.S. and around the world—didn't understand what was happening. They compounded the crisis by imposing tax increases, making a bad situation spectacularly worse. Governments thought balancing their budgets would restore confidence and so they hit their economies with higher taxes.

The United States, for example, in 1932 passed a bill of astonishing tax hikes. Income tax rates were raised exponentially, with the top rate more than doubling, to 63%. A stamp tax on checks accelerated the economy's downward spiral by pushing people to withdraw cash from banks already struggling. There were absurd and nonsensical increases of excise taxes on items such as candy and movie tickets.

Things were nearly as bad in Great Britain, which raised income taxes in 1930 and again in 1931. The Germans were especially hard hit by the trade war and responded with a battery of taxes that deepened the slump.

Floundering and confused, many governments then turned to debasing their money by going off the gold standard, led by Great Britain in late 1931. Britain got a brief boost by devaluing the pound, but not for long. After London's devaluation, at least 20 countries quickly followed suit. The United States did the same in 1934, as did Italy and Belgium; France finally devalued the franc in 1936. These beggar-thy-neighbor devaluations, as they were called, were ultimately damaging to the global economy. In the end there were no winners. The 1930s ended up as a lost decade economically. The terrible slump led to the Second World War. The experience compelled allied and neutral nations to convene in Bretton Woods, New Hampshire, in 1944 and create a new gold-based international monetary system.

Monetary expert Lawrence White further points out that the economic crisis between the first and second World Wars was not due to nations being on the gold standard, "It was due to many countries *leaving* the gold standard, inflating massively while *off* the gold standard, and then resuming the gold standard at the *old parity* (not devaluing to accommodate a higher price level)."

Myth: *A gold standard would be vulnerable to attacks by speculators.* Reality: *This can't happen if nations know how to defend their currencies by increasing or decreasing their monetary base to maintain a stable value.*

In today's giant global markets, where traders have access to sophisticated computer technology and vast resources, wouldn't a gold-based monetary system be vulnerable to speculative attack? The famous example offered by gold naysayers is the attack more than two decades ago led by financier George Soros on the pound, which was then tied to the German mark. With the value of the pound sinking on worldwide currency exchanges, Soros and his fellow speculators launched a massive short sale of the pound, dumping so many on the market that Great Britain was forced to raise interest rates. Eventually it had to sever the tie to the mark and float the pound. Soros and others ultimately pocketed billions in profits.

A gold-based dollar—or any currency—can withstand this kind of attack if nations know how to "defend" their currencies by maintaining their value. Example: In 2009, Russia thwarted an attack on the ruble by buying its own currency. Shrinking the monetary base maintained the ruble's value. With its immense assets, the United States could easily defend against an attack on a gold-backed dollar by similarly shrinking its monetary base.

In 1992, the Bank of England could have maintained Britain's fix to the Deutschmark if it had sold bonds, thereby reducing the supply of pounds. Britain had more than ample resources to beat back the speculators—but it didn't know how to do it.

Myth: *Setting a fixed gold/dollar ratio constitutes price fixing.*
Reality: *A fixed gold/dollar ratio is necessary for money to fulfill its function as a measure of value.*

Whether the price of gold is $35 an ounce, $300—or beyond—a set gold/dollar ratio isn't price fixing. The gold price anchors the dollar so that it can fulfill its function as one of society's weights and measures. We have explained before that, just as a ruler measures space, money measures value. The dollar's value in gold can no more vary than the number of inches in a ruler can change every week. All weights and measures are "fixed." The same should be true of money, which is the economy's most fundamental measuring instrument.

Myth: *Setting a new gold/dollar ratio is dangerous.*
Reality: *Not if you set a ratio that maintains present-day values and prices.*

Subscribers to this myth often give the example of the deflation that roiled Great Britain in 1925 as the reason why gold won't work. That's like saying your computer doesn't work when the real problem is that you loaded it with outdated, decade-old software. Of course it won't work. The same was true of the Brits' 1925 return to their pre-World War I gold/pound ratio. They were essentially reloading their system based on outdated values, though wartime inflation had more than doubled the cost of living.

Their deflationary trauma could have been avoided had the pound been pegged to gold based on higher post-war values. The British government compounded the error by not lowering its high wartime taxes. This also depressed the economy.

For a gold standard to work, the dollar—or, for that matter the pound or the euro—must have a gold price that takes into account the current cost of living. Thus, even the reasonable-sounding $370 price of gold that prevailed in the late 1980s and '90s would today be too low. But what if the price of gold becomes inflated by investor anxiety, as it was several years ago and is to some extent today? This was especially true in 2011 at the very height of Quantitative Easing, when anxiety over that unprecedented monetary expansion and fears of inflation and a possible U.S. government bond default created a gold-buying frenzy that drove the price to historic highs. Answer: the dollar's gold price should only be set after careful calculations, taking into account forward markets in gold, the price of inflation-protected bonds, and the 10-year average price of gold. It's important to then mark up that gold price to avoid a low ratio that could cause a drop in nominal wages. The mathematical formulas can vary. But the objective must be a realistic gold price that will restore certainty and get the economy moving again. An example of a country that did get it right: France, which, unlike 1920s Britain, took into account post-World War I inflation, and correctly pegged the franc to gold. Also unlike Britain, France reformed its tax system in the mid-1920s, especially by reducing its top income tax rate from 60% to 30%. Combined with the realistic gold/franc ratio, France prospered and avoided Britain's economic travails of the era.

The Bottom Line

We have said this before: There is no perfect system. But the inherent soundness and stability of gold is our best hope of ending the volatility and serial crises of today's markets.

CHAPTER 14

Bringing Back America

THIS BOOK HAS MAPPED OUT A ROAD TO AN AMERICAN Revival that can be achieved by removing the foremost barriers to growth and prosperity: Obamacare, the federal income tax code, and the Federal Reserve. The problems in healthcare, taxes, and monetary policy are the biggest obstacles to a real recovery—and the biggest threats to our future as a democratic, free society. Reform these three vital areas and the dreary stagnation of the Obama years will at last become a bad memory.

This will be good for us and for the world. When America gets things right, the world tends to follow. After Ronald Reagan set the U.S. back on the road to prosperity in the 1980s, over 50 countries followed our example. Commerce flourished as taxes and trade restrictions were lowered. The global economy enjoyed a nearly quarter-century long boom. The Reagan years were a triumph not only for economic but political freedom.

We don't need another Ronald Reagan for a great American comeback. We need an administration that understands and will act on Reagan's ideas, which are, after all, American principles with us since the founding of our Republic. This does not mean slavishly imitating Reagan's specific polices. It means enacting reforms based on the Reaganite belief that a true American revival can only come from the ingenuity of people in free markets—not

161

from rigid top-down policies imposed by government bureaucrats and self-interested politicians.

Let's briefly review the steps to take now.

Repeal Obamacare

Contrary to supporters' expectations, this miserable legislation is just as unpopular today as when it was rammed through Congress by Barack Obama. Far from solving the very real problems in healthcare, it has made a bad situation dangerously worse. Instead of getting "affordable healthcare," Americans have been slammed by skyrocketing premiums and deductibles and paltry insurance coverage with narrow networks, in addition to an increasingly bad physician shortage and longer waits to see a doctor. Countless rules and bureaucratic constraints—including the top-down Electronic Health Records mandate—have taken critical decisions out of the hands of physicians and are driving them out of the practice of medicine.

Given the horrors visited upon so many of our veterans by government-controlled Veterans Administration hospitals, it's hard to imagine how anyone, regardless of their political affiliation, could think that more government is the answer for healthcare. Yet Obamacare inflicts the same kind of constraints and bureaucracy on American medicine.

There is no getting around it: to fix what's ailing American healthcare, *Obamacare must be repealed.* Americans need a medical system where the patient is truly in charge. The problem with healthcare is that the system is currently dominated by third parties—government, employers, and private insurance companies. Real healthcare must return control to you, the individual patient. To achieve this requires not only repealing Obamacare but making other critical changes. They include:

- *Require that healthcare providers, particularly hospitals and clinics, post prices for all procedures and services.* This will encourage consumers to shop for healthcare as they do for other products and services, spurring competition among providers of care that will lower prices.
- *Create a national market for insurance and larger risk pools by allowing consumers to shop for coverage across state lines.*
- *Equal tax treatment, allowing both individuals and employers to receive tax deductions for buying health insurance.* This would begin to turn the destructive system of third-party pay into a patient-driven healthcare market.
- *Remove Obamacare's costly coverage mandates.* We can begin to dismantle Obamacare by eliminating its coverage mandates that require policies to include a raft of benefits— whether the individual wants them or not. Eliminating these cost-inflating mandates would bring down the cost of premiums. While we're at it, the medical device tax and other Obamacare levies should be scrapped.
- *Encourage the growth of tax-free health savings accounts.* Health savings accounts (HSAs) are IRA-like accounts that enable you to set aside tax-free dollars to pay for healthcare. Under current law, you and your employer are permitted to make tax-free contributions to your HSA. But the amounts of permissible contributions are limited; those ceilings should be removed or substantially raised.
- *Current federal spending on Medicaid should be given to the states as grants.* Let states decide what works best for their residents.

These and other reforms discussed in this book will create a patient-driven market for both care and insurance. Doctors, hospitals and insurers wanting to attract your business will lower prices and improve the quality and attentiveness of care. We'll finally get a healthcare system that works!

Implement the Flat Tax

The federal income tax code is an incomprehensible monstrosity. Its enormous waste of time, money, and brainpower is a drag on the economy. The code has corrupted behavior throughout society, especially in Washington. Requiring more than 80,000 agents for tax collection and enforcement, the gargantuan tax code has made the IRS into a feared government agency that increasingly— and criminally—abuses its power and threatens the freedom of Americans as never before. That's why we need drastic reform. Replacing the tax code with a Flat Tax so that you could literally fill out your return on a single sheet of paper or with a few minutes on your computer would eliminate the complexity and loopholes that give power to Washington's armies of lobbyists and bureaucrats. It would ignite an exciting and vibrant economy where jobs and opportunities to move up the income ladder would be plentiful.

Reform the Federal Reserve

With a handful of exceptions, policymakers, politicians, commentators, and economists remain astonishingly ignorant of the immense damage this agency is doing to the U.S. and global economies. The Federal Reserve System was founded more than a century ago to be the lender of last resort to the banking system. Since the Nixon Administration in 1971 severed the dollar's link to gold, a link that gave the greenback a fixed value, the Federal Reserve has increasingly treated monetary policy and financial regulations like a Soviet-style central planning bureaucracy would. The resulting fluctuating "fiat" dollar has produced a marked increase in major financial crises—including the 2008 financial meltdown, a result of the subprime mortgage mania enabled by the Fed's weak dollar policies. The Fed's weakening of the dollar over time is also eroding the wealth of hundreds of millions of Americans. A new threat to our financial system, and our freedom, is now coming from the Fed's expanding regulatory authority over non-bank institutions like insurance companies.

The Federal Reserve as it operates today violates the basic tenet of money: to function, it must have a fixed and stable value. Money, as we explain in Part 3, is similar to a yardstick: it measures value just as a yardstick measures distance. No one thinks that the Bureau of Weights and Measures should manipulate the number of inches in a foot or the number of ounces in a pound. Nor should the Fed be in the business of manipulating the value of money, the economy's foremost measure of value.

A return to a healthy economy requires that the Federal Reserve's power be cut down to size. No more artificially low interest rates and hyper-regulation of banks. The Fed's mission should be mainly to preserve a sound and stable dollar. As for the dollar itself, the best route to stability is to restore its link to gold. Ultimately, we must create a new gold standard, which served this country well for 180 years, from the time of George Washington's presidency to the early 1970s.

The reforms in this book are the first steps to restoring the economic and social health of this nation and bringing about a true American Revival. Will the politicians listen? That depends on you.

Notes

Introduction

1   *the Great Recession officially ended in 2009*   The National Bureau of Economic Research, U.S. Business Cycle Expansions and Contractions, September 20, 1010, http://www.nber.org/cycles.html, accessed October 13, 2015.

1   *some 60% of Americans feel that the economy is still in decline*   Gallup, "Weekly U.S. Economic Confidence Index Falls to 11-Month Low," by Justin McCarthy, September 1, 2015, http://www.gallup.com/poll/185177/weekly -economic-confidence-index-falls-month-low.aspx, accessed October 13, 2015.

1   *since 2009 Americans have seen a sharp decline in real incomes . . . the biggest drop has been experienced by the bottom 20% of income earners*   National Employment Law Project, "Occupational Wage Declines Since the Great Depression," September 2015, http://www.nelp.org/content/uploads/Occupational-Wage -Declines-Since-the-Great-Recession.pdf, accessed October 13, 2015.

2   *the labor participation rate—which reflects the number of people who have dropped out of the workplace—is the lowest in decades*   Bureau of Labor Statistics, Data Tools, undated, http://data.bls.gov/timeseries/LNS11300000, accessed October 13, 2015.

2   *sending naval vessels to the edge of U.S. waters*   *Wall Street Journal*, "Chinese Navy Ships Came Within 12 Nautical Miles of U.S. Coast," by Jeremy Page and Gordon Lubold, September 4, 2015, http://www.wsj.com/articles/chinese -navy-ships-off-alaska-passed-through-u-s-territorial-waters-1441350488, accessed October 14, 2015.

2   *constructing man-made islands in a disputed area of the South China Sea*   *Wall Street Journal*, "China's Unchallenged Sea Grab," August 26, 2015, http://www .wsj.com/articles/chinas-unchallenged-sea-grab-1440628992, accessed October 14, 2015.

3   *healthcare, which makes up almost 20% of our economy*   Centers for Medicare & Medicaid Services, "National Health Expenditure Data—Historical," undated, https://www.cms.gov/research-statistics-data-and-systems/statistics-trends -and-reports/nationalhealthexpenddata/nationalhealthaccountshistorical .html, accessed October 14, 2015.

167

4   *World War II regulations and a 1954 change in our tax law*   National Bureau of Economic Research, "Employer-Sponsored Health Insurance and The Promise of Health Insurance Reform," by Thomas C. Buchmueller and Alan C. Monheit, April 2009, http://www.nber.org/papers/w14839.pdf, accessed October 14, 2015.

4   *Indonesia (home to the world's largest population of Muslims)*   Pew Research Center, "Muslim Population of Indonesia," November 4, 2010, http://www.pewforum.org/2010/11/04/muslim-population-of-indonesia/, accessed October 14, 2015.

5   *America had a gold standard for most of its history*   Nathan Lewis, *Gold: The Once and Future Money* (John Wiley & Sons, 2007), p. 155.

5   *among his proposals was a 30% cut in income tax rates for everyone. Reagan promised to end the seemingly incurable inflation . . . He also proposed the biggest peacetime military buildup ever*   The American Presidency Project, "Address Before a Joint Session of the Congress on the Program for Economic Recovery," Speech by President Ronald Reagan, February 18, 1981, http://www.presidency.ucsb.edu/ws/?pid=43425, accessed October 14, 2015.

5   *landslide victory in 1980*   U.S. National Archives and Records Administration, http://www.archives.gov/federal-register/electoral-college/map/historic.html #1980, accessed October 14, 2015.

5   *stabilizing the dollar, he killed debilitating inflation once and for all. His massive income tax cuts*   Cato Institute, "Supply-Side Tax Cuts and the Truth about the Reagan Economic Record," by William A. Niskanen and Stephen Moore, October 22, 1996, http://object.cato.org/sites/cato.org/files/pubs/pdf/pa261.pdf, accessed October 14, 2015.

5   *a decade after his ascendency to the White House, the Soviet Union lay in tatters and had ceased to exist*   U.S. Department of State, "The Collapse of the Soviet Union," modified October 31, 2013, https://history.state.gov/milestones/1989-1992/collapse-soviet-union, accessed October 14, 2015.

6   *their unfunded liabilities now run into the tens of trillions of dollars*   Social Security Administration, "The 2015 Annual Report of the Board of Trustees of the Federal Old-Age And Survivors Insurance and Federal Disability Insurance Trust Funds," July 22, 2015, http://www.ssa.gov/oact/tr/2015/tr2015.pdf, accessed October 13, 2015; Centers for Medicare & Medicaid Services, "2015 Annual Report of The Boards of Trustees of The Federal Hospital Insurance and Federal Supplementary Medical Insurance Trust Funds," July 22, 2015, https://www.cms.gov/Research-Statistics-Data-and-Systems/Statistics-Trends -and-Reports/ReportsTrustFunds/Downloads/TR2015.pdf, accessed October 13, 2015; *Wall Street Journal*, "Medicare by the Scary Numbers," by John C. Goodman and Laurence J. Kotlikoff, June 24, 2013, http://www.wsj.com/articles/SB10001424127887323393804578555461959256572, accessed October 13, 2015.

6   *the Nazis received only 2% of the vote in 1928*   United States Holocaust Memorial Museum, "The Holocaust: A Learning Site for Students," http://www.ushmm.org/outreach/en/article.php?ModuleId=10007671, accessed October 13, 2015.

Chapter 1 Why Healthcare Today Is Such a Mess

12   Time *magazine recounted the case of a man who lost his insurance*   *Time*, "When Health Insurance Isn't Health Insurance," by Karen Tumulty, June 16, 2009, http://swampland.time.com/2009/06/16/when-health-insurance-isnt-health -insurance/, accessed September 21, 2015.

12   *David Goldhill adds up what a typical American will pay for medical care*   David Goldhill, *Catastrophic Care: Why Everything We Think We Know about Health Care Is Wrong* (Vintage Books, 2013), pp. 59–60.

13   *we still produce more new drugs and medical devices than the rest of the world* SelectUSA, "The Pharmaceutical and Biotech Industries in the United States," undated, http://selectusa.commerce.gov/industry-snapshots/pharmaceutical-and -biotech-industries-united-states.html, accessed September 21, 2015; SelectUSA, "The Medical Device Industry in the United States," undated, http://selectusa .commerce.gov/industry-snapshots/medical-device-industry-united-states, accessed September 21, 2015.

13   *a sector that represents 18% of our economy*   Centers for Medicare & Medicaid Services, "National Health Expenditure Data—Historical," undated, https:// www.cms.gov/research-statistics-data-and-systems/statistics-trends-and -reports/nationalhealthexpenddata/nationalhealthaccountshistorical.html, accessed September 21, 2015.

13   *each year tens of thousands of patients die from secondary infections*   Centers for Disease Control and Prevention, "Healthcare-associated Infections (HAIs)," undated, http://www.cdc.gov/HAI/surveillance/, accessed September 21, 2015.

14   *instead, seniors today spend a greater proportion of their retirement income* American Federation of State, County and Municipal Employees, "Mandatory Medicare Assignment for Physicians," June 25–29, 1990, http://www.afscme.org/ members/conventions/resolutions-and-amendments/1990/resolutions/42 -mandatory-medicare-assignment-for-physicians, accessed September 24, 2015.

16   *Kaiser Permanente, the Geisinger Health System, and a handful of other institutions have been lauded*   David Goldhill, *Catastrophic Care: Why Everything We Think We Know about Health Care Is Wrong* (Vintage Books, 2013), p. 328.

16   *reimbursements depend not on performance but rather how hospitals negotiate* Merrill Matthews, The Institute for Policy Innovation, correspondence.

17   *a reason widely overlooked is that Medicare doesn't reimburse for such tools because they weren't used back in 1965*   Slate.com, "Please Hold for the Doctor," Melissa Jayne Kinsey, June 26, 2014, http://www.slate.com/articles/technology/future_ tense/2014/06/telemedicine_e_visits_doctors_should_start_using_email .html, accessed October 25, 2015.

17   *in the early 1900s, an automobile cost the equivalent today of some $125,000*   The Henry Ford, "Transportation: Past, Present and Future," undated, http://www .thehenryford.org/education/erb/TransportationPastPresentAndFuture.pdf, accessed September 21, 2015.

17   *along came Henry Ford, who, along with a gifted group of engineers*   Ford, "Game Changer: 100th Anniversary Of The Moving Assembly Line," September 12, 2013, https://media.ford.com/content/fordmedia/fna/us/en/features/game -changer--100th-anniversary-of-the-moving-assembly-line.html,   accessed September 21, 2015.

18   *in 2009, then senior White House advisor David Axelrod himself admitted*   CNN, "President Obama Set to Deliver Health Care Reform Address; Plane Hijacked in Mexico, " September 9, 2009, http://www.cnn.com/TRANSCRIPTS/0909/09/ sitroom.03.html, accessed September 21, 2015.

18   *a 2014 report released by the American Medical Association (AMA) found that 72%*   American Medical Association, "10 top states where health insurers dom-

inate: New study," October 9, 2014, http://www.ama-assn.org/ama/ama-wire/
post/10-top-states-health-insurers-dominate-new-study, accessed September 21,
2015.

18   *in more than half the states in the U.S., anyone who wants to build a new hospital*   National Conference of State Legislatures, "Certificate of Need: State Health
Laws And Programs," September 2015, http://www.ncsl.org/research/health/con
-certificate-of-need-state-laws.aspx, accessed September 21, 2015.

19   *a medium-sized acute care facility in San Diego, California*   John C. Goodman
and Gerald L. Musgrave, Patient Power: Solving America's Health Care Crisis,
(Cato Institute, 2013), p. 290, http://www.ncpa.org/pub/patient-power, accessed
September 2015.

19   *to get a single drug approved by the FDA takes about 10 years*   The Institute
for Policy Innovation, "The High Cost of Inventing New Drugs—And of Not
Inventing Them," by Merrill Matthews, April 16, 2015, http://www.ipi.org/
ipi_issues/detail/the-high-cost-of-inventing-new-drugs-and-of-not-inventing
-them-2, accessed September 24, 2015.

19   *back in 2004, a groundbreaking a study by Duke University's Christopher Conover*
Cato Institute, "Health Care Regulation: A $169 Billion Hidden Tax," by
Christopher Conover, October 4, 2004, http://www.cato.org/publications/policy
-analysis/health-care-regulation-$169-billion-hidden-tax, accessed September
24, 2015.

20   *millions have had the procedure done*   Federal Trade Commission, "The Basics
of LASIK Eye Surgery," undated, http://www.consumer.ftc.gov/articles/0062
-basics-lasik-eye-surgery, accessed September 24, 2015.

20   Forbes *magazine publisher Rich Karlgaard paid $5,000 for Lasik*   Rich Karlgaard,
Forbes magazine publisher.

20   *demand has grown more than six-fold in the last two decades*   National
Center for Policy Analysis, "Why Can't The Market for Medical Care Work
Like Cosmetic Surgery?," by Devon Herrick, June 17, 2013, http://healthblog
.ncpa.org/why-cant-the-market-for-medical-care-work-like-cosmetic-surgery/,
accessed September 25, 2015.

20   *the NBER in March 2015 studied the impact of what are called consumer-directed
health plans (CDHP) over a three-year period*   National Bureau of Economic
Research, "Do 'Consumer-Directed' Health Plans Bend the Cost Curve Over
Time?," by Amelia M. Haviland, Matthew D. Eisenberg, Ateev Mehrotra, Peter J.
Huckfeldt, and Neeraj Sood, March 2015, http://www.nber.org/papers/w21031.
pdf, accessed September 24, 2015.

21   *an HSA is a tax-free IRA-like account which you can get from your employer*   The
Council for Affordable Health Insurance, "HSAs, FSAs, HRAs: Which
Consumer-Driven Health Care Option Should You Choose?," undated, http://
www.cahi.org/cahi_contents/resources/pdf/n124HSAFSAHRASeptember2011
.pdf, accessed September 24, 2015.

21   *according to the NBER's study, "Spending is reduced for those in firms offering
CDHPs*   Haviland, Eisenberg, Mehrotra, Huckfeldt, and Sood, op. cit.

21   *employers . . . turned to offering fringe benefits—like health insurance*   National
Bureau of Economic Research, "Employer-Sponsored Health Insurance and the
Promise of Health Insurance Reform," by Thomas C. Buchmueller and Alan C.

Monheit, April 2009, http://www.nber.org/papers/w14839, accessed September 21, 2015.

21   *after the war, Washington formally allowed employers to treat these insurance outlays as a tax-deductible expense while not treating them as taxable income for workers*   Ibid.

21   *In the 1960s . . . establishment of Medicare and Medicaid*   Centers for Medicare & Medicaid Services, "History," undated, https://www.cms.gov/About-CMS/Agency-Information/History/index.html?redirect=/History/, accessed September 21, 2015.

Chapter 2 How Obamacare Made the Situation Worse and Not Better

23   *former Democratic Speaker of the House Nancy Pelosi's now infamous insistence that we had to pass Obamacare to know what's in it*   Washington Post, "Pelosi Defends Her Infamous Health Care Remark," by Jonathan Capehart, June 20, 2012, http://www.washingtonpost.com/blogs/post-partisan/post/pelosi-defends-her-infamous-health-care-remark/2012/06/20/gJQAqch6qV_blog.html, accessed October 5, 2015.

23   *led to some 63 House members losing their seats in the 2010 election*   New York Times, Election Results—House Map, undated, http://elections.nytimes.com/2010/results/house, accessed September 22, 2015.

23   *half of the senators who voted for the bill subsequently also lost their jobs*   Washington Examiner, "Half of the Senators Who Voted for Obamacare Won't Be Part of New Senate," by Philip Klein, December 6, 2014, http://www.washingtonexaminer.com/25-senators-who-voted-for-obamacare-wont-be-part-of-new-senate/article/2555721, accessed September 22, 2015.

24   *46 million people in the U.S. who were uninsured*   White House, "The Economic Case for Health Care Reform, undated, https://www.whitehouse.gov/administration/eop/cea/TheEconomicCaseforHealthCareReform/, accessed September 22, 2015.

24   *the billion-dollar federal website Healthcare.gov*   Americans for Tax Reform, "Healthcare.Gov to Cost Taxpayers over $1 billion," by John Kartch and Ryan Ellis, May 19, 2014, https://www.atr.org/healthcaregov-cost-taxpayers-over-1-billion, accessed September 22, 2015.

24   *"if you like your health care plan you can keep your health care plan"*   White House, "Health Insurance Reform Reality Check," undated, https://www.whitehouse.gov/assets/documents/Health_Insurance_Reform_PDF_1.pdf, accessed September 22, 2015.

24   *millions of people had to scramble to get coverage*   Health Affairs Blog, "How Many Nongroup Policies Were Canceled? Estimates from December 2013," by Lisa Clemans-Cope and Nathaniel Anderson, March 3, 2014, http://healthaffairs.org/blog/2014/03/03/how-many-nongroup-policies-were-canceled-estimates-from-december-2013/, accessed September 22, 2015.

24   *its health insurance exchanges may provide lots of subsidies to pay premiums*   The Henry J. Kaiser Family Foundation, "Health Insurance Marketplace Calculator," undated, http://kff.org/interactive/subsidy-calculator/, accessed September 22, 2015.

24   *the annual rise in the cost of health services has increased from less than 4% a year to almost 6%*   Forbes.com, "Health Costs Resume Their Rise," by Sally Pipes, May 5, 2014, http://www.forbes.com/sites/sallypipes/2014/05/05/health-costs-resume-their-rise/, accessed September 22, 2015; Forbes.com, "The Coming Healthcare Inflation," by Scott Gottlieb, August 6, 2015, http://www.forbes.com/sites/scottgottlieb/2015/08/06/the-coming-healthcare-inflation/, accessed September 22, 2015.

25   *the infamous tax on medical devices*   Internal Revenue Service, "Medical Device Excise Tax: Frequently Asked Questions," February 3, 2014, http://www.irs.gov/uac/Medical-Device-Excise-Tax:-Frequently-Asked-Questions, accessed September 22, 2015

25   *Obamacare's employer mandate, requiring that companies with over 50 employees pay for their health care*   FreedomWorks, "2015 Brings ObamaCare Employer Mandate," by Tom Borelli, January 7, 2015, http://www.freedomworks.org/content/2015-brings-obamacare-employer-mandate, accessed September 22, 2015.

25   *a 2014* Washington Post-*ABC News Survey of 1,000 adults*   Washington Post, "April 2014 *Washington Post*-ABC News Poll: Obama, Politics 2014 Congressional Elections," May 1, 2014, http://www.washingtonpost.com/page/2010-2019/WashingtonPost/2014/04/29/National-Politics/Polling/release_342.xml, accessed September 22, 2015.

25   *the $2.7 trillion that the law is expected to cost over the next ten years*   Michael Tanner, *Bad Medicine: A Guide to the Real Costs and Consequences of the New Health Care Law* (Cato Institute, 2011), p. 30, http://object.cato.org/sites/cato.org/files/pubs/pdf/BadMedicineWP.pdf, accessed September 22, 2015.

25   *analyst Scott Atlas cites a 2014 study that found that "an estimated 71% of the new insurance arises through Medicaid*   CNN, "How Obamacare Fails the Poor and Middle Class," by Scott W. Atlas, March 4, 2015, http://www.cnn.com/2015/03/04/opinion/atlas-obamacare-poor-middle-class/, accessed September 22, 2015.

25   *38% of physicians limit the number of Medicaid patients they'll treat*   The Institute for Policy Innovation, "Doctors Face a Huge Medicare and Medicaid Pay Cut in 2015," by Merrill Matthews, January 5, 2015, http://www.ipi.org/ipi_issues/detail/doctors-face-a-huge-medicare-and-medicaid-pay-cut-in-2015, accessed September 22, 2015.

26   *healthcare analyst John Graham of the National Center for Policy Analysis similarly says*   National Center for Policy Analysis, "New Evidence That Obamacare Is Working?," by John R. Graham, July 31, 2015, http://healthblog.ncpa.org/new-evidence-that-obamacare-is-working/, accessed September 22, 2015.

26   Forbes *contributor Paul Hsieh and others have pointed out that Obamacare in various ways is creating incentives to control health care costs by "undertreatment rather than overtreatment"*   Forbes.com, "How ObamaCare Creates Ethical Conflicts For Physicians and How Patients Can Protect Themselves," by Paul Hsieh, January 28, 2014, http://www.forbes.com/sites/paulhsieh/2014/01/28/how-obamacare-creates-ethical-conflicts-for-physicians/, accessed September 22, 2015.

26   *plans offered on the health insurance exchanges created by the Affordable Care Act include 34% fewer providers*   Avalere, "Exchange Plans Include 34

Percent Fewer Providers than the Average for Commercial Plans," by Chris Sloan and Elizabeth Carpenter, July 15, 2015, http://avalere.com/expertise/managed-care/insights/exchange-plans-include-34-percent-fewer-providers-than-the-average-for-comm, accessed September 23, 2015.

27   *some on these plans have had to travel considerable distances to see those physicians*   Fox News, "ObamaCare patients may encounter fewer doctors, longer wait times," by Jim Angle, February 11, 2014, http://www.foxnews.com/politics/2014/02/11/obamacare-patients-may-encounter-fewer-doctors-longer-wait-times/, accessed September 22, 2014.

27   *she had to drive 400 miles to see the nearest doctor covered under her plan*   KTEN .com, "Cancer Survivor Encounters Problems with Obamacare," May 28, 2014, http://www.kten.com/story/25636763/cancer-survivor-encounters-problems-with-obamacare?clienttype=generic&mobilecgbypass; accessed October 13, 2015.

27   *Frank Alfisi, a 73-year-old retired produce seller*   The American Spectator, "Obamacare Takes a Life, " by Jeffrey Lord, April 1, 2014, http://spectator.org/articles/58588/obamacare-takes-life, accessed September 22, 2015; Centers for Medicare and Medicaid Services, "Fact Sheet: Two Midnight Rule," July 1, 2015, https://www.cms.gov/Newsroom/MediaReleaseDatabase/Fact-sheets/2015-Fact-sheets-items/2015-07-01-2.html, accessed September 22, 2015.

27   *"physician extenders" who are not M.D.s, are increasingly administering care*   Forbes.com, "Paging Physician Assistants as Obamacare Fuels Demand," Bruce Japson, February 22, 2015; http://www.forbes.com/sites/brucejapsen/2015/02/22/paging-physician-assistants-as-obamacare-fuels-demand/, accessed October 13, 2015.

28   *the actress Janine Turner said that when her father was admitted*   PJ Media, "My Father and Hospitalists, " by Janine Turner, June 13, 2014, http://pjmedia.com/blog/my-father-and-hospitalists/2/, accessed September 22, 2015.

28   *in 2015, Medicare announced that it would pay for end-of-life counseling*   New York Post, "Look Out, Grandma: Uncle Sam Is Selling 'Death with Dignity,'" by Betsy McCaughey, July 13, 2015, http://betsymccaughey.com/look-out-grandma-uncle-sam-is-selling-death-with-dignity/, accessed September 22, 2015.

29   *the Department of Health and Human Services promised that Obamacare would help "expand the number of primary-care doctors, nurses, and physician assistants"*   Pacific Research Institute, "Obamacare Will Make U.S. Doctor Shortage Worse," by Sally C. Pipes, May 7, 2015, http://www.pacificresearch.org/article/obamacare-will-make-us-doctor-shortage-worse/, accessed September 22, 2015.

29   *2015 study by the Association of American Medical Colleges projects a shortfall of up to 90,000 physicians in the U.S. by 2025*   Association of American Medical Colleges, "New Physician Workforce Projections Show the Doctor Shortage Remains Significant," March 3, 2015, https://www.aamc.org/newsroom/news releases/426166/20150303.html, accessed September 22, 2015

29   *commentator Charles Krauthammer, who has an M.D. in psychiatry, noted that classmates at his medical school's 40th reunion*   Washington Post, "Why Doctors Quit," by Charles Krauthammer, May 28, 2015, https://www.washingtonpost .com/opinions/why-doctors-quit/2015/05/28/1e9d8e6e-056f-11e5-a428-c984eb077d4e_story.html, accessed September 22, 2015.

29   *a study in the* American Journal of Emergency Medicine *found that doctors in the ER spend the bulk of their time—43%—entering electronic records information,*

28% with patients   The American Journal of Emergency Medicine, "4000 Clicks: a productivity analysis of electronic medical records in a community hospital ED," by Robert G. Hill Jr., Lynn Marie Sears, and Scott W. Melanson, September 23, 2013, http://www.ajemjournal.com/article/S0735-6757%2813%2900405-1/abstract, accessed September 22, 2015.

30   *can get paid as little as $25 for a visit*   New York Times, "As Medicaid Payments Shrink, Patients Are Abandoned," by Kevin Sack, March 15, 2010, http://www.nytimes.com/2010/03/16/health/policy/16medicaid.html?_r=1, accessed September 23, 2015.

30   *doctors today now see nearly twice the number of patients*   Wall Street Journal, "Why Doctors Are Sick of Their Profession," by Sandeep Jauhar, August 29, 2014, http://www.wsj.com/articles/the-u-s-s-ailing-medical-system-a-doctors-perspective-1409325361, accessed September 23, 2015.

30   *Obamacare's cost pressures are also destroying once-lucrative private practices, forcing many doctors into large, impersonal groups based in hospitals*   Wall Street Journal, "ObamaCare's Threat to Private Practice," by Scott Gottlieb, December 7,2014,http://www.wsj.com/articles/scott-gottlieb-obamacares-threat-to-private-practice-1417990367, accessed September 23, 2015.

30   *the Cato Institute's Michael Tanner laments, "Medicine is simply no longer the profession that it once was"*   Cato Institute, "Obamacare: Fewer Doctors, More Demand," by Michael Tanner, September 10, 2014, http://www.cato.org/publications/commentary/obamacare-fewer-doctors-more-demand, accessed September 22, 2015.

30   *in 2008, candidate Barack Obama promised that his administration's health care reform would save families $2,500 a year on health insurance premiums*   Wall Street Journal Blogs, "Parsing Obama's Promise to Lower Insurance Premiums by $2,500," by Jacob Goldstein, July 23, 2008, http://blogs.wsj.com/health/2008/07/23/parsing-obamas-promise-to-lower-insurance-premiums-by-2500/, accessed September 23, 2015.

30   *since Obamacare was passed, insurance premiums have gone up and deductibles have risen sharply*   The Henry J. Kaiser Family Foundation, "2015 Employer Health Benefits Survey," September 22, 2015, http://kff.org/report-section/ehbs-2015-summary-of-findings/, accessed September 23, 2015.

31   *the millions of Americans initially kicked off their health insurance when the act went into effect in 2014*   Clemans-Cope and Anderson, op. cit.

31   *typical was the experience of 56-year-old Arkansas mom Wanda Buckley*   Forbes .com, "Obamacare Canceled My Health Plan, And Increased My Premiums By 50 Percent, But At Least I'll Have Maternity Care," by Wanda Buckley and Avik Roy, April 30, 2014, http://www.forbes.com/sites/theapothecary/2014/04/30/obamacare-canceled-my-health-plan-and-increased-my-premiums-by-50-percent-but-at-least-ill-have-maternity-care/, accessed September 23, 2015.

31   *in 2015, a study of healthcare benefits and spending by the actuarial firm Milliman*   Milliman, "2015 Milliman Medical Index, by Christopher S. Girod, Scott A. Weltz, and Susan K. Hart, May 19, 2015, http://us.milliman.com/mmi/, accessed September 23, 2015.

31   *Grace-Marie Turner of the Galen Institute wrote in USA Today*   USA Today, "Families brace for steep hikes: Opposing view," by Grace-Marie Turner, August 11, 2015,   http://www.usatoday.com/story/opinion/2015/08/11/affordable-care-act

-health-insurance-premiums-editorials-debates/31480355/, accessed September 24, 2015.

32   *healthcare analyst Sally Pipes, "Obamacare covers high-risk individuals in the most expensive way possible*   Pacific Research Institute, "Obamacare Will Wreck U.S. Taxpayers, So Here's Another Plan," by Sally C. Pipes, October 14, 2013, http://www.pacificresearch.org/article/obamacare-will-wreck-us-taxpayers-so-heres-another-plan/, accessed September 23, 2015.

32   *under the law's age rating restrictions, an insurer can't charge a 64-year old a rate that is more than three times what it charges a 21-year old for the same plan*   Heritage   Foundation,   "Obamacare   and   Insurance   Rating   Rules: Increasing Costs and Destabilizing Markets," by Edmund F. Haislmaier, January 20,   2011,   http://www.heritage.org/research/reports/2011/01/obamacare-and-insurance-rating-rules-increasing-costs-and-destabilizing-markets,   accessed September 24, 2015.

32   *before Obamacare, insurance premiums were rising because of state mandates*   National Center for Policy Analysis, "The Cost of Health Insurance Mandates," by John C. Goodman and Merrill Matthews, August 13, 1997, http://www.ncpa.org/pub/ba237,   accessed   September   23,   2015;   Commonwealth Foundation, "New Mandates A Step Backwards in Health Care Reform," by Nathan Benefield,   July   2,   2008,   http://www.commonwealthfoundation.org/research/detail/new-mandates-a-step-backwards-in, accessed September 23, 2015.

32   *healthcare analysts such as Sally Pipes believe that Obamacare's perverse incentives will continue to drive up costs*   Pipes, op. cit.

32   *Sean Parnell of the Heartland Institute writes*   Heartland Institute, "Millennials' Health Insurance Premiums Skyrocket Under Obamacare," by Sean Parnell, May   13,   2015,   http://news.heartland.org/newspaper-article/2015/05/18/millennials-health-insurance-premiums-skyrocket-under-obamacare,   accessed September 23, 2015; Heritage Foundation, "2015 ACA-Exchange-Premiums Update: Premiums Still Rising," by Drew Gonshorowski, March 20, 2015, https://www.heartland.org/sites/default/files/ib4366.pdf, accessed September 23, 2015.

33   *according to a study by the firm HealthPocket, the average deductible*   Health Pocket, "2015 Obamacare Deductibles Remain High But Don't Grow Beyond 2014 Levels,"   November   2014,   https://www.healthpocket.com/healthcare-research/infostat/2015-obamacare-deductible-copayment-coinsurance-out-of-pocket#.VgbMLK7kExd, accessed September 22, 2015.

33   *more than 70% of metro areas have "highly concentrated" health insurance markets*   American Medical Association, "10 Top States Where Health Insurers Dominate: New Study, " October 9, 2014, http://www.ama-assn.org/ama/ama-wire/post/10-top-states-health-insurers-dominate-new-study, accessed September 24, 2015.

34   *CNNMoney.com reported in 2014: "Overall U.S. unemployment has fallen steeply*   CNN Money, "Part-Time Jobs Put Millions in Poverty or Close to It," by Patrick Gillespie, November 20, 2014, http://money.cnn.com/2014/11/20/news/economy/america-part-time-jobs-poverty/, accessed September 23, 2015.

34   *Obamacare's estimated $569 billion in new or increased taxes and fees*   Tanner, op. cit.

35   *accurately measured, the Patient Protection and Affordable Care Act will cost more than $2.7 trillion*   Ibid.

35   *in 2014, Dr. Scott Atlas wrote in the* Wall Street Journal   *Wall Street Journal,* "ObamaCare's Anti-Innovation Effect," by Scott W. Atlas, October 1, 2014, http://www.wsj.com/articles/scott-w-atlas-obamacares-anti-innovation-effect-1412204490, accessed September 22, 2015.

36   *the device tax his company paid last year exceeded his company's entire R&D budget*   Ibid.

Chapter 3   What to Do Now: Steve's Plan for Revolutionizing Healthcare

37   *DNA sequencing is giving rise to . . . personalized medicine*   ARK Invest Research, "Disruptive Innovation: New Markets, New Metrics," by Catherine Wood and Arthur Laffer, September 2015.

37   *to date, some 268,000 human genomes have been sequenced*   Ibid.

38   *sequencing a human genome cost $10 million*   Nature, "The $1,000 Genome," by Erika Check Hayden, March 19, 2014, http://www.nature.com/news/technology-the-1-000-genome-1.14901#/falling, accessed October 14, 2015.

38   *today it costs $1,000*   Personalized Medicine Coalition, "Personalized Medicine by the Numbers," http://www.personalizedmedicinecoalition.org/Userfiles/PMC-Corporate/file/pmc_personalized_medicine_by_the_numbers.pdf, accessed October 14, 2015.

38   *she cites the example of tests for thyroid cancer*   ARK Investment Management, "Why This Bull Market May Continue to Surprise," by Catherine Wood, August 18, 2015, http://research.ark-invest.com/this-bull-market-may-continue-to-surprise, accessed September 24, 2015.

39   *even though it has grown more than sixfold over the past 20 years*   Time, "These 3 Trends Are Changing the Face of Plastic Surgery," by Eliza Gray, April 30, 2015, http://time.com/3842179/plastic-surgery-trends/, accessed September 25, 2015.

39   *conventional laser eye surgery*   National Center for Policy Analysis, "Why Can't The Market for Medical Care Work Like Cosmetic Surgery?," by Devon Herrick, June 17, 2013, http://healthblog.ncpa.org/why-cant-the-market-for-medical-care-work-like-cosmetic-surgery/, accessed September 25, 2015.

41   *a study by healthcare economists at the University of Minnesota*   Cato Institute, "Cato Handbook for Policymakers, 7th Edition," undated, http://object.cato.org/sites/cato.org/files/serials/files/cato-handbook-policymakers/2009/9/hb111-16.pdf, accessed September 24, 2015.

41   *some are already offering "multi-state" insurance plans*   Health Affairs Blog, "Implementing Health Reform: Multi-State Plan Program; Benefits and Payment Rule, Letter to Issuers to Follow," by Timothy Jost, February 20, 2015, http://healthaffairs.org/blog/2015/02/20/implementing-health-reform-multi-state-plan-program-benefits-and-payment-rule-letter-to-issuers-to-follow/, accessed September 25, 2015.

41   *such alliances have the potential over time to create a national market*   http://www.forbes.com/sites/theapothecary/2012/05/11/will-buying-health-insurance-across-state-lines-reduce-costs/, accessed September 24, 2015.

41   *multi-state plans should become available in all states by 2017*   Jost, op. cit.

42   *the employer-based market for health insurance came about following the tax deduction*   National Bureau of Economic Research, "Employer-Sponsored Health Insurance and the Promise of Health Insurance Reform," by Thomas C.

Buchmueller and Alan C. Monheit, April 2009, http://www.nber.org/papers/w14839.pdf, accessed September 24, 2015.

43   *Consumer Operated and Oriented Plans [CO-OPS]—non-profit cooperatives that are favorite of progressives—have been a failure*   Galen Institute, "Letter to Congress Re: Co-ops," by Joel C. White and Grace-Marie Turner, September 11, 2015, http://www.galen.org/2015/letter-to-congress-re-co-ops/, accessed September 24, 2015

43   *removing coverage diktats could lower premium costs as much as 44 percent for*   Heritage Foundation, "Responding to King v. Burwell: Congress's First Step Should Be to Remove Costly Mandates Driving Up Premiums," by Edmund F. Haislmaier and Drew Gonshorowski, May 4, 2015, http://www.heritage.org/research/reports/2015/05/responding-to-king-v-burwell-congresss-first-step-should-be-to-remove-costly-mandates-driving-up-premiums, accessed September 24, 2015.

43   *in 2015, most people were allowed to contribute up to $3,350 for individuals or up to $6,650 for families*   Internal Revenue Service, "26 CFR 601.602: Tax Forms and Instructions," undated, http://www.irs.gov/pub/irs-drop/rp-14-30.pdf, accessed September 24, 2015.

43   *where the worker can lose money that hasn't been spent by year's end*   Internal Revenue Service, "Modification of "Use-or-Lose" Rule For Health Flexible Spending Arrangements (FSAs)," undated, http://www.irs.gov/pub/irs-drop/n-13-71.pdf, accessed September 24, 2015.

44   *and if you use the money for non-medical expenses, you will find yourself liable*   Internal Revenue Service, "Publication 969," undated, http://www.irs.gov/publications/p969/ar02.html#en_US_2014_publink1000204081, accessed September 24, 2015.

44   *the number of HSAs and health reimbursement arrangements increased some 150% from 2008*   Employee Benefit Research Institute, "Health Savings Accounts and Health Reimbursement Arrangements: Assets, Account Balances, and Rollovers, 2006–2014," by Paul Fronstin and Anne Elmlinger, January 2015, http://www.ebri.org/pdf/briefspdf/EBRI_IB_409_Jan15_CEHCS.pdf, accessed September 25, 2015.

44   *total account balances came to more than $22 billion*   Employee Benefit Research Institute, "Health Savings Accounts and Health Reimbursement Arrangements: Assets, Account Balances, and Rollovers, 2006–2010," by Paul Fronstin, January 2011, http://www.ebri.org/pdf/briefspdf/IB.Jan11.CEHCS.FinalFlow.03Jan11.pdf, accessed September 25, 2015.

44   *the proportion of people covered by employer plans using these types of accounts*   Mercer, "Modest Health Benefit Cost Growth Continues as Consumerism Kicks Into High Gear," November 19, 2014, http://www.mercer.com/newsroom/modest-health-benefit-cost-growth-continues-as-consumerism-kicks-into-high-gear.html#5, accessed September 25, 2015.

45   *current law allows employees to contribute up to $2,500 a year tax free*   "Modification of "Use-or-Lose" Rule For Health Flexible Spending Arrangements (FSAs)," op. cit.

46   *there was a U.S. District Court decision in 1979*   *Wall Street Journal*, "Small Slice of Doctors Account for Big Chunk of Medicare Costs," by Christopher Weaver, Tom McGinty and Louise Radnofsky, April 9, 2014, http://www.wsj.com/articles/

small-slice-of-doctors-account-for-big-chunk-of-medicare-costs-1397015936, accessed September 24, 2015.

47   *insurers must spend 80%–85% of premiums on reimbursements*   American Legislative Exchange Council, "The State Legislators Guide to Repealing ObamaCare," 2011, http://www.alec.org/wp-content/uploads/State_Leg_Guide _to_Repealing_ObamaCare.pdf, accessed September 24, 2015.

47   *Independent Payment Advisory Board, the Obamacare bureaucracy*   White House, "The Facts About the Independent Payment Advisory Board," by Nancy-Ann Deparle, April 20, 2011, https://www.whitehouse.gov/blog/2011/04/20/ facts-about-independent-payment-advisory-board, accessed September 24, 2015.

Chapter 4 Why We Need Radical Tax Reform Now

51   *the way the British decided to tax tea so enraged Bostonians that they swarmed British ships, tossing crates of the stuff into Boston Harbor*   History.com, "Boston Tea Party," undated, http://www.history.com/topics/american-revolution/ boston-tea-party, accessed October 15, 2015.

52   *Abraham Lincoln's Gettysburg Address, which defined the character of the American nation, was all of 272 words*   Cornell University Library, "The Gettysburg Address," http://rmc.library.cornell.edu/gettysburg/good_cause/transcript.htm, accessed October 13, 2015.

52   *the Declaration of Independence, about 1,300 words*   Telegram.com, "Tax Code Beats 'em All in Word Count," http://www.telegram.com/article/20111110/ LETTERS/111109108/1055. Posted November 10, 2011, accessed October 13, 2015.

52   *the Holy Bible, which took centuries to put together, 773,000 words*   Ibid.

52   *the federal income tax code and all its attendant rulings and interpretations has been estimated to be about 10 million words and rising*   Tax Foundation, "Federal Tax Laws and Regulations are Now Over 10 Million Words Long," by Scott Greenberg, October 8, 2015, http://taxfoundation.org/blog/federal-tax -laws-and-regulations-are-now-over-10-million-words-long, accessed October 25, 2015.

52   *even Barack Obama has called for simplifying this mess*   The White House, "A Simpler, Fairer Tax Code That Responsibly Invests in Middle Class Families," (Press Release) January 17, 2015. https://www.whitehouse.gov/the-press-office/ 2015/01/17/fact-sheet-simpler-fairer-tax-code-responsibly-invests-middle -class-fami, accessed October 13, 2015.

53   *several years ago,* Money *magazine*   Money, "6 Mistakes Even the Tax Pros Make," by Joan Caplin, March, 1998.

53   *take they hypothetical case of "Richard"*   The Wire.Cutter.com, "The Best Tax Software," by Kevin Purdy, March 16, 2015, http://thewirecutter.com/reviews/ best-tax-software/#human, accessed October 27, 2015.

53   *taxpayer Paul Hatz*   DailyFinance.com, "Tax Audit Horror Stories: When the IRS Attacks," by Ross Kenneth Urken, February 28, 2012, http://www .dailyfinance.com/2012/02/28/tax-audit-horror-stories-irs, accessed September 24, 2015.

54   *government contractor Glen Wiggy went to Iraq in 2008*   TheWeek.com, "Tax-time Horror Stories: 6 Mistakes to Avoid," by Natasha Burton, March 8, 2015, http://theweek.com/articles/542936/taxtime-horror-stories-6-mistakes-avoid, accessed September 24, 2015.

54   *contrary to what the left frequently claims, the top 1% of income earners pay* more *than their fair share. They accounted for nearly half* CNBC.com, "Top 1% pay nearly half of federal income taxes," Robert Frank, April 14, 2015, http://www .cnbc.com/2015/04/13/top-1-pay-nearly-half-of-federal-income-taxes.html, accessed September 24, 2015.

55   *Warren Buffett famously complained* CNN Money, "Buffett Says He's Still Paying Lower Tax Rate Than His Secretary," by Chris Isidore, March 4, 2013, http://money.cnn.com/2013/03/04/news/economy/buffett-secretary-taxes/, accessed September 24, 2015.

55   *"[T]he evolution of business lobbying from a sparse reactive force into a ubiquitous and increasingly proactive one is among the most important transformations in American politics over the last 40 years."* The Atlantic, April 20, 2015, http://www.theatlantic.com/business/archive/2015/04/how-corporate-lobbyists -conquered-american-democracy/390822/, accessed September 24, 2015.

56   *while less than $2 billion is needed to run the national legislature* Ibid.

56   *the Mercatus Center puts the annual cost of compliance as high as $378 billion and pegged the total annual economic cost (including work hours) at more than $600 billion* Mercatus Research, "The Hidden Costs of Tax Compliance," by Jason J. Fichtner and Jacob M. Feldman, May 20, 2013, http://mercatus.org/sites/default/ files/Fichtner_TaxCompliance_v3.pdf, accessed September 24, 2015.

57   *federal revenue increased by 62%* The Heritage Foundation, "The Historical Lessons of Lower Tax Rates," by Daniel J. Mitchell, August 13, 2003, http://www .heritage.org/research/reports/2003/08/the-historical-lessons-of-lower-tax -rates, accessed September 24, 2015.

57   *federal revenue soared during the Reagan era* White House OMB, history chart, https://www.whitehouse.gov/sites/default/files/omb/budget/fy2016/assets/ hist01z1.xls, accessed September 24, 2015.

57   *President Ronald Reagan instituted an across-the-board income tax cut that lowered rates by 23% . . . Another round of cuts in 1986 reduced the top income tax rate from 50% to 28%* CNN Money, "What People Forget About Reagan," by Jeanne Sahadi, September 12, 2010, http://money.cnn.com/2010/09/08/news/economy/ reagan_years_taxes/, accessed September 24, 2015.

57   *the national net wealth increased by $17 trillion, 10 times the increase in the national debt* Forbes.com, "Reagan's Century," by Rich Karlgaard, December 13, 1999, http://www.forbes.com/forbes/1999/1213/6414051a.html, accessed September 24, 2015.

58   *and a net increase of 16.1 million new jobs between 1983 and 1989* Forbes.com, "Sorry, Obama Fans: Reagan Did Better on Jobs and Growth," by Kyle Smith, September 11, 2014, http://www.forbes.com/sites/kylesmith/2014/09/11/sorry -obama-fans-reagan-did-better-on-jobs-and-growth/, accessed September 24, 2015.

58   *a 1% hike in the personal income tax rate translates into a reduction in real GDP per capita of up to approximately 3% . . . "If it came down 10 points—still higher than most of our trading partners—it would add 1 to 2 points to GDP growth and likely not lose tax revenue"* The Tax Foundation, "What Is the Evidence on Taxes and Growth?" by William McBride, December 18, 2012, http://taxfoundation.org/article/what-evidence-taxes-and-growth, accessed September 24, 2015.

59   *Khalid Quran* Wall Street Journal, The IRS Ill-Gotten Gains, (Editorial), July 15, 2015, http://www.wsj.com/articles/the-irss-ill-gotten-gains-1437001667, accessed October 13, 2015.

59   *Maryland dairy farmer Randy Sowers had more than $62,000 seized*   Ibid.

59   *the IRS engaged in some 600 forfeitures before public outcry forced the agency to pull back*   Ibid.

60   *there have been more than 15,000 changes to the code*   PolitiFact.com, "Sen. Rob Portman Says Hundreds of Tax Preferences and Loopholes Have Been Added Since 1986," by Stephen Koff, March 11, 2013, http://www.politifact.com/ohio/statements/2013/mar/11/rob-portman/sen-rob-portman-says-hundreds-tax-preferences-and-/, accessed September 24, 2015.

Chapter 5   What Is a Flat Tax?

62   *we saw that with the 1986 reforms, which consisted of two rates*   The Free Dictionary, "Tax Reform Act of 1986, undated, http://legal-dictionary.the freedictionary.com/Tax+Reform+Act+of+1986, accessed September 25, 2015.

62   *they've since multiplied into the seven*   Forbes.com, "IRS Announces 2015 Tax Brackets, Standard Deduction Amounts And More," by Kelly Phillips Erb, October 30, 2014, http://www.forbes.com/sites/kellyphillipserb/2014/10/30/irs-announces-2015-tax-brackets-standard-deduction-amounts-and-more/, accessed September 25, 2015.

62   *this $52,800 threshold, by the way, is more than double the current federal poverty level*   ObamaCare Fact, "Federal Poverty Level," http://obamacarefacts.com/federal-poverty-level/, accessed September 25, 2015.

62   *the EITC . . . can amount to an additional subsidy of more than $6,200*   IRS.gov, "2015 EITC Income Limits, Maximum Credit Amounts and Tax Law Updates," https://www.irs.gov/Credits-&-Deductions/Individuals/Earned-Income-Tax-Credit/EITC-Income-Limits-Maximum-Credit-Amounts-Next-Year, accessed October 13, 2015.

63   *taxpayers start out with a $4,000 personal exemption*   Forbes.com, Kelly Phillips Erb, op. cit.

65   *John Dunham & Associates, a highly regarded economic research firm . . . Congressional Budget Office now forecasts*   American Enterprise Institute, "The Revenue and GDP Impact of the Perry Flat Tax Plan—Now With Actual Numbers!" James Pethokoukis, October 26, 2011, http://www.aei.org/publication/the-revenue-and-gdp-impact-of-the-perry-flat-tax-plan-now-with-actual-numbers/print/, accessed September 25, 2015.

67   *the United States' putative corporate taxes have encouraged the emergence of "transfer pricing"*   Forbes.com, "Transfer Pricing as Tax Avoidance," Lee Sheppard, posted 6/25/2010, http://www.forbes.com/2010/06/24/tax-finance-multinational-economics-opinions-columnists-lee-sheppard.html, accessed October 13, 2015.

67   *General Electric incurred political wrath in 2011 when it reported global profits of $14.2 billion, claiming that only $5.1 billion of those profits were generated in the United States*   New York Times, "G.E.'s Strategies Let It Avoid Taxes Altogether," by David Kocieniewski, March 24, 2011, http://www.nytimes.com/2011/03/25/business/economy/25tax.html, accessed September 25, 2015.

68   *when the dividend tax was cut from 38% to 15% in 2003*   National Center for Policy Analysis, "Benefits of the Bush Dividend Tax Cut," by Bruce Bartlett, August 27, 2004, http://www.ncpa.org/pub/ba483, accessed September 25, 2015.

69   *median incomes are lower than they were in 2007—and far lower than their peak in 1999*   Wikipedia.org, "Household income in the United States," https://en

.wikipedia.org/wiki/Household_income_in_the_United_States,   accessed
September 25, 2015.

69   *President Obama signed into law a number of tax increases, including a top mar-*
      ginal tax rate of 39.6%   Newsmax, "Taxpayers Face New 39.6 Percent Bracket
      as New Rates Kick In," January 22, 2014, http://www.newsmax.com/Newsfront/
      US-SPE-Taxes-Overview/2014/01/22/id/548285/, accessed October 13, 2015.

69   *and economy-killing hikes in capital gains taxes from 15 to nearly 24% (the rate*
      includes a 3.8% investment tax levied under Obamacare)   Americans For Tax
      Reform, "Full List of Obama Tax Hikes," http://www.atr.org/full-list-ACA-tax
      -hikes-a6996, accessed October 13, 2015.

Chapter 6 Thriving Under the Flat Tax

71   *the United States would join more than 40 nations or jurisdictions that have*
      adopted this system. . . . Among these are Russia, Romania, Lithuania, Hong
      Kong, Ukraine, and Hungary   Flat Tax: Essays on the Adoption and Results of
      the Flat Tax Around the Globe, "Countries or Jurisdictions with a Flat Tax as
      of March 2015," by Alvin Rabushka, March 20, 2015, http://flattaxes.blogspot
      .com/2015/03/countries-or-jurisdictions-with-flat_20.html, accessed September
      27, 2015

72   *the first to enact a Flat Tax in 1947*   Heritage Foundation, "Flat Tax is
      the Way of the Future," by Daniel J. Mitchell, March 20, 2006, http://www
      .heritage.org/research/commentary/2006/03/flat-tax-is-the-way-of-the-future,
      accessed September 27, 2015.

72   *a former British colony, it was turned over to China as special administrative*
      region in 1997   CIA World Factbook, Hong Kong, updated September 24, 2015,
      https://www.cia.gov/library/publications/the-world-factbook/geos/hk.html,
      accessed September 28, 2015.

72   *Hong Kong offers residents a choice: They can pay taxes under a traditional sys-*
      tem of four graduated tax rates, ranging from 2% to 17%   GovHK, "Tax Rates of
      Salaries Tax & Personal Assessment, " undated, http://www.gov.hk/en/residents/
      taxes/taxfiling/taxrates/salariesrates.htm, accessed September 27, 2015.

72   *these include deductions for charitable contributions and interest payments on*
      home loans   GovHK, "Deductions," undated, http://www.gov.hk/en/residents/
      taxes/salaries/allowances/deductions/index.htm, accessed September 28, 2015.

72   *as well as allowances for children, married couples, and dependents*   GovHK,
      "Basic and Other Allowances," undated, http://www.gov.hk/en/residents/taxes/
      salaries/allowances/allowances/index.htm, accessed September 28, 2015.

72   *they can opt to pay the "Standard Rate," a 15% Flat Tax, if they fall into a higher*
      bracket   GovHK, Tax Rates of Salaries & Personal Assessment, op. cit.

72   *the standard rate is paid by a tiny percentage of high-income residents. But it*
      accounts for a substantially larger percentage of total tax revenue   Cato Institute,
      "Hong Kong's Excellent Taxes, " by Alan Reynolds, June 2, 2005, http://www.cato
      .org/publications/commentary/hong-kongs-excellent-taxes, accessed September
      28, 2015.

72   *corporate tax rate of 16.5% and an even lower rate of 15% for small busi-*
      nesses   GovHK, Press Release, Speech by Financial Secretary, October 9, 2014,
      http://www.info.gov.hk/gia/general/201410/09/P201410090595.htm,   accessed
      September 28, 2015.

72   *427 square miles in size and with slightly more than 7 million residents*   CIA World Factbook, op. cit.

72   *it has the ninth highest GDP per capita, according to the International Monetary Fund; it has suffered only one year of negative economic growth since the turn of the century*   International Monetary Fund, World Economic Outlook Database.

73   *Hong Kong recently surpassed the United States in foreign direct investment, and is now second in world behind China, bringing in more than $100 billion in 2014*   United Nations Conference on Trade and Development, World Investment Report 2015, http://unctad.org/en/PublicationsLibrary/wir2015_en.pdf, accessed September 28, 2015.

73   *before it enacted a Flat Tax in 2001*   Hoover Institution, "The Flat Tax at Work in Russia: Year Three," by Alvin Rabushka, April 26, 2004, http://www.hoover.org/research/flat-tax-work-russia-year-three, accessed September 29, 2015.

73   *in the early 2000s, newly elected President Vladimir Putin began enacting crucial economic reforms*   Peterson Institute for International Economics, "An Assessment of Putin's Economic Policy," by Anders Aslund, July 2008, http://www.piie.com/publications/papers/paper.cfm?ResearchID=974, accessed September 29, 2015.

73   *in the first year under the Flat Tax, government revenues increased by a whopping 25%, accounting for inflation, and rose again by the same percentage in 2002. By the end of 2004, revenues had more than doubled*   Hoover Institute, "The Flat Tax at Work in Russia: Year Four, 2004," by Alvin Rabushka, January 26, 2005, http://www.hoover.org/research/flat-tax-work-russia-year-four-2004, accessed September 29, 2015.

73   *Russia claims more billionaires than any other country except the U.S., China, Germany and India*   Forbes.com, "Inside the 2015 *Forbes* Billionaires List: Facts and Figures," by Kerry A. Dolan and Luisa Kroll, March 2, 2015, http://www.forbes.com/sites/kerryadolan/2015/03/02/inside-the-2015-forbes-billionaires-list-facts-and-figures/, accessed September 29, 2015.

73   *"Russia is a good place to be if you are rich"*   Russia Beyond the Headlines, "Can Russia be a Tax Haven for Wealthy Europeans?," by Elizaveta Surnacheva, Grigory Tumanov, Vera Sitnina, Alexei Tarkhanov, February 1, 2013, http://rbth.com/society/2013/02/01/can_russia_be_a_tax_haven_for_wealthy_europeans_22415.html, accessed September 28, 2015.

73   *Gérard Depardieu, disgusted with France's 75% tax under socialist President Francois Hollande, chucked his French passport and embraced Russian citizenship*   New York Times, "That Russian Movie Star, Gérard Depardieu," by David Herszenhorn, January 3, 2013, http://www.nytimes.com/2013/01/04/world/europe/putin-makes-gerard-depardieu-a-citizen-of-russia.html,   accessed September 29, 2015; Tax Foundation, "France's 75 Percent Tax Rate Offers a Lesson in Revenue Estimating," May 28, 2014, http://taxfoundation.org/blog/france-s-75-percent-tax-rate-offers-lesson-revenue-estimating, accessed September 29, 2015.

74   *there has been at least one proposal by the center-left Fair Russia party to impose a 30% tax on high earners*   Forbes.com, "Russia Considers Going Progressive... When It Comes to Tax, " by Kelly Phillips Erb, July 22, 2014, http://www.forbes.com/sites/kellyphillipserb/2014/07/22/russia-considers-going-progressive-when-it-comes-to-tax/, accessed September 29, 2015.

74   *Estonia . . . was the first to enact a Flat Tax. Its 26% flat tax on business and personal incomes*   Cato Institute, "The Global Flat Tax Revolution," by Daniel J. Mitchell, July/August 2007, http://www.cato.org/policy-report/julyaugust-2007/global-flat-tax-revolution, accessed September 29, 2015.

74   *less than a decade later, the country's economy had become the second-fastest growing in Europe, after neighboring Latvia, which also instituted a Flat Tax*   International Monetary Fund, op. cit.

74   *Estonia understands the importance of keeping a single low tax rate and has, in fact, reduced it to 20%*   European Union, "Income Taxes Abroad—Estonia," Updated June 23, 2015, http://europa.eu/youreurope/citizens/work/taxes/income-taxes-abroad/estonia/index_en.htm, accessed September 29, 2015.

74   *Estonia also flattened the corporate income tax*   Flat Tax: Essays on the Adoption and Results of the Flat Tax Around the Globe, by Alvin Rabushka, March 26, 2007, http://flattaxes.blogspot.com/2008/11/estonia-plans-to-reduce-its-flat-tax.html, accessed September 29, 2015.

74   *Estonia ranks high on the Heritage Foundation/Wall Street Journal Index of Economic Freedom*   Heritage Foundation, 2015 Index of Economic Freedom, Estonia, http://www.heritage.org/index/country/estonia, accessed September 29, 2015.

74   *Estonia drew nearly $1 billion in foreign investment in 2014 alone*   United Nations, op. cit.

75   *Estonia has more startups per capita than any European state*   Wall Street Journal, "The Many Reasons Estonia Is a Tech Start-Up Nation," by Ben Rooney, June 14, 2012, http://www.wsj.com/articles/SB10001424052702303734204577464343888754210, accessed September 29, 2015.

75   *Skype got its start there*   Microsoft, "Skype at 10: How an Estonian Startup Transformed Itself (and the World)," undated, http://www.microsoft.com/en-us/stories/skype/skype-chapter-2-welcome-to-estonia.aspx, accessed September 29, 2015.

75   *Wi-Fi is almost always free*   Visit Estonian, "Wifi in Estonia," undated, http://www.visitestonia.com/en/things-to-know-about-estonia/facts-about-estonia/wifi-in-estonia, accessed September 29, 2015.

75   *the country has been a model of "e-government"*   The Atlantic, "Lessons From the World's Most Tech-Savvy Government," by Sten Tamkivi, January 24, 2014, http://www.theatlantic.com/international/archive/2014/01/lessons-from-the-worlds-most-tech-savvy-government/283341/, accessed September 29, 2015.

75   *in 2012 [Paul Krugman] enraged Estonians by snipping at the tiny nation for an "incomplete recovery"*   New York Times Blog, "Estonian Rhapsody," by Paul Krugman, June 6, 2012, http://krugman.blogs.nytimes.com/2012/06/06/estonian-rhapsdoy/, accessed September 29, 2015.

75   *Estonia cut civil servants' salaries 10% and the pay of its government ministers 20%*   The Guardian, "Estonia and Latvia: Europe's Champion of Austerity," by Josephine Moulds, June 8, 2012, http://www.theguardian.com/world/2012/jun/08/estonia-latvia-eurozone-champions-austerity, accessed September 29, 2015.

75   *Dan Mitchell deftly pointed out on Forbes.com*   Forbes.com, "Estonia and Austerity: Another Exploding Cigar for Paul Krugman," by Daniel J. Mitchell, June 7, 2012, http://www.forbes.com/sites/danielmitchell/2012/06/07/estonia

-and-austerity-another-exploding-cigar-for-paul-krugman/, accessed September 29, 2015.

75   *President Toomas Ilves, taking to Twitter, called the* New York Times *columnist "smug, overbearing and patronizing"* Bloomberg, "Krugmenistan vs. Estonia," by Brendan Greely, July 20, 2012, http://www.bloomberg.com/bw/articles/2012-07-19/krugmenistan-vs-dot-estonia, accessed September 29, 2015.

75   *Latvian composer Eugene Birman to immortalize the feud in* Nostra Culpa NPR, "New Opera Immortalizes Spat Between Paul Krugman, Estonian President," by January 21, 2013, http://www.npr.org/2013/01/21/169920880/new-opera-immortalizes-spat-between-paul-krugman-estonian-president, accessed September 29, 2015; *Wall Street Journal* Blog, "Ilves—Krugman Spat to be Turned Into 'Financial Opera'," by Liis Kangsepp, January 10, 2013, http://blogs.wsj.com/emergingeurope/2013/01/10/ilves-krugman-spat-to-be-turned-into-financial-opera/, accessed September 29, 2015.

75   *"Professor Krugman was pontificating on a matter that he had no authority to discuss, but this has worked for us and we're not so much interested in what you have to say"* NPR, op. cit.

76   *inflation as high as 958% in 1992* U.S. Library of Congress, "Postindependence Economic Difficulties," undated, http://countrystudies.us/latvia/19.htm, accessed September 29, 2015.

76   *Latvia was one of the earliest proponents of the Flat Tax, instituting the policy in 1995* Hoover Institution, "The Flat Tax's Silver Anniversary," by Alvin Rabushka, 2007, http://www.hoover.org/sites/default/files/flat_tax_silver_anniversary.pdf, accessed September 29, 2015.

76   *personal income in Latvia is taxed at 23% and corporate income and capital gains are taxed at 15%* Ministry of Finance Republic of Latvia, Tax System in Latvia, undated, http://www.fm.gov.lv/en/s/taxes/, accessed September 29, 2015; KPMG, Corporate Tax Rates Table, undated, https://home.kpmg.com/xx/en/home/services/tax/tax-tools-and-resources/tax-rates-online/corporate-tax-rates-table.html, accessed September 29, 2015.

76   *since implementing the Flat Tax, Latvia has grown at a rate that is often the fastest in the European Union* International Monetary Fund, op. cit.

76   *25% by 1995* U.S. Department of State, "1995 Country Reports on Economic Policy and Trade Practices: Latvia," January 20, 2001, http://1997-2001.state.gov/www/issues/economic/trade_reports/russia_nis95/latvia.html, accessed September 29, 2015.

76   *by 2014, Latvia, which has adopted the euro, had an inflation rate of less than 1%* European Union, "Latvia and the Euro," updated November 21, 2014, http://ec.europa.eu/economy_finance/euro/countries/latvia_en.htm, accessed September 29, 2015; Heritage Foundation, 2015 Index of Economic Freedom, Latvia, http://www.heritage.org/index/country/latvia, accessed September 29, 2015.

76   *Lithuania initially instituted a Flat Tax rate of 33% in 1994* Economist, "The Case for Flat Taxes," April 14, 2005, http://www.economist.com/node/3860731, accessed October 10, 2015; KPMG, Tax Card 2015 With Effect From 1 January 2015 Lithuania, https://www.kpmg.com/LV/lv/IssuesAndInsights/ArticlesPublications/Publicationseries/nodoklu-publikacijas/Documents/LT-Tax-Card-Eng-2015.pdf.

77   *experienced a sharp, temporary downturn in growth during the global reces-
     sion*   International Monetary Fund, op. cit.

77   *Hungary instituted a 16% Flat Tax in January 2011. With corporate taxes under
     20%*   National Tax and Customs Administration, "Guidelines, Summaries
     on   Taxation,"   undated,   http://en.nav.gov.hu/taxation/taxinfo/summary_
     individuals.html, accessed September 29, 2015.

77   *which was contracting, instantly began to revive, reaching a high of 4% growth in
     2014*   International Monetary Fund, op. cit.

77   *will lower its rate to 15% in 2016*   Hungary Today, "Economy Minister Hails Tax
     Reduction as 2016 Budget Bill Submitted to Parliament," May 14, 2015, http://
     hungarytoday.hu/news/economy-minister-hails-tax-reduction-2016-budget
     -bill-submitted-parliament-20567, accessed September 29, 2015.

77   *tax code that involved five separate rates as high as 40%*   Hoover Institute, "The
     Flat Tax Spreads to Romania," by Alvin Rabushka, January 3, 2005, http://www
     .hoover.org/research/flat-tax-spreads-romania, accessed September 29, 2015.

77   *an estimated one-third of the nation's economic activity*   Bank Austria
     Creditanstalt, "Romania: Catching Up Process with Hurdles," by Jan Stankovsky,
     March   2004,   http://www.bankaustria.at/informations   pdfs/BEL_XPLICIT_
     RUMAENIEN.pdf, accessed September 29, 2015.

77   *Traian Băsescu won the presidency after running on a flat tax platform*   Rabushka,
     "The Flat Tax Spreads to Romania," op. cit.

77   *just two years later, economic growth averaged 7.8% rate over a three-year period
     from 2006 to 2008*   International Monetary Fund, op. cit.

77   *has helped attract investment—$3.2 billion last year*   United Nations, op. cit.

78   *Georgia joined the global Flat Tax fraternity in December 2004, passing the Flat
     Tax into law by a large margin*   Flat Tax: Essays on the Adoption and Results of
     the Flat Tax Around the Globe, "The Flat Tax Spreads to Georgia," January 3, 2005,
     http://flattaxes.blogspot.com/2008/11/flat-tax-spreads-to-georgia-january-3
     .html, accessed September 29, 2015.

78   *the economy shot up from less than 6% growth to more than 12% growth in
     2007*   International Monetary Fund, op. cit.

78   *Russian invasion of Georgia in 2008, which caused South Ossetia and Abkhazia
     to break away and become Russian satellites*   CNN.com, "2008 Georgia Russia
     Conflict Fast Facts," updated April 12, 2015, http://www.cnn.com/2014/03/13/
     world/europe/2008-georgia-russia-conflict/, accessed September 29, 2015.

78   *just one year of negative growth in 2009, and rising quickly back to pre-
     recession growth levels almost immediately, to more than 6% in 2010*   International
     Monetary Fund, op. cit.

78   *Greece's progressive tax system has rates going up to 42%*   European Union,
     "Income Taxes Abroad: Greece," updated July 15, 2015, http://europa.eu/your
     europe/citizens/work/taxes/income-taxes-abroad/greece/index_en.htm,
     accessed September 29, 2015.

78   *Bulgaria and Macedonia each have a simple 10% Flat Tax*   Rabushka, March 20,
     2015, op. cit.

78   *Albania abandoned the Flat Tax*   Flat Tax: Essays on the Adoption and Results
     of the Flat Tax Around the Globe, "Albania Abandons Its Flat Tax," by Alvin
     Rabushka, December 29, 2013, http://flattaxes.blogspot.com/2013/12/albania
     -abandons-its-flat-tax.html, accessed September 29, 2015.

78   *Slovakia abandoned the Flat Tax*   European Politics and Policy, "Slovakia Has Abolished its Flat Tax Rate, but Other Eastern and Central European Countries are Likely to Continue with the Policy," by Andreas Peichi, March 18, 2013, http://blogs.lse.ac.uk/europpblog/2013/03/18/slovakia-abandon-flat-tax/, accessed September 29, 2015.

79   *economic growth reached 7.5% after Albania implemented a flat tax of 10 percent in 2008*   International Monetary Fund, op. cit.; Rabushka, December 29, 2013, op. cit.

79   *after the socialists triumphed in the country's 2013 election*   Ibid.

79   *five tax brackets, some 90 different exemptions, along with two different VATs*   Tax Foundation, "Flat Tax Lessons From Slovakia," by Scott A. Hodge, October 26, 2011, http://taxfoundation.org/blog/flat-tax-lessons-slovakia, accessed September 29, 2015.

79   *in 2003, the Slovak parliament enacted a Flat Tax of 19%*   Hoover Institute, "The Flat Tax Spreads to Slovakia," by Alvin Rabushka, November 3, 2003, http://www.hoover.org/research/flat-tax-spreads-slovakia, accessed September 2015.

79   *dramatic increase in foreign direct investment, especially from auto manufacturers like Hyundai-Kia*   U.S. Department of State, "2013 Investment Climate Statement—Slovakia," April 2013, http://www.state.gov/e/eb/rls/othr/ics/2013/204731.htm, accessed September 2015.

79   New York Times *dubbed Slovakia "The Detroit of Europe"*   New York Times, "Slovakia's Automakers Skirt Crisis for Now," by William J. Kole, November 30, 2008, http://www.nytimes.com/2008/11/30/business/worldbusiness/30iht-motown.4.18267689.html?pagewanted=all, accessed September 29, 2015.

79   *in 2013, Slovakia's newly elected leftist government ditched the Flat Tax in favor of a "directly progressive income tax" with higher rates*   Peichi, op. cit.

79   *in 2014, economic growth was only 2.4%*   International Monetary Fund, op. cit.

Chapter 7   Why the Flat Tax Is a Better Alternative than a Consumption Tax

81   *Jeb Bush wants to reduce the seven brackets down to three low tax rates of 28%, 25% and 10%*   Jeb 2016, undated, https://jeb2016.com/backgrounder-jeb-bushs-tax-reform-plan/, accessed October 1, 2015.

81   *the corporate tax rate would be slashed from 35% to 20%*   Ibid.

81   *Marco Rubio has proposed a plan with two rates, 15% and 35%. That 35% isn't much lower than the 39.6% top rate under the Obama Administration*   Tax Foundation, "Presidential Hopeful Marco Rubio Already has a Tax Plan," by Kyle Pomerleau, April 14, 2015, http://taxfoundation.org/blog/presidential-hopeful-marco-rubio-already-has-tax-plan, accessed October 1, 2015.

81   *a cut in the corporate tax rate from 35% to 25%*   Ibid.

81   *eliminates the capital gains tax and personal income taxes on dividends and interest*   Senator Marco Rubio, "Economic Growth and Family Fairness Tax Reform Plan," undated, http://www.rubio.senate.gov/public/index.cfm/files/serve/?File_id=2d839ff1-f995-427a-86e9-267365609942, accessed October 1, 2015.

81   *full expensing of business investment and no more taxes on business income already taxed abroad*   Pomerleau, op. cit.

82   *like the Bush plan, Rubio would send the death tax to the grave*   Rubio, op. cit.

82   *Chris Christie advocates a Reagan-style plan based on three rates with a top rate of 28% . . . lower the corporate rate to 25% and encourage corporations to repatriate overseas profits with a low, one-time levy of 8.75%*   Wall Street Journal, "Gov. Chris Christie Pushes for Reagan-Era Tax Rates," by John D. McKinnon and Bob Davis, May 12, 2015, http://www.wsj.com/articles/gov-chris-christie-pushes-for-reagan-era-tax-rates-1431473784, accessed October 1, 2015.

82   *Donald Trump's plan—10%, 20%, and 25%*   DonaldTrump.com, "Tax Reform That Will Make America Great Again," https://www.donaldjtrump.com/positions/tax-reform, accessed October 13, 2015.

82   *Dr. Ben Carson is the only one to propose a flat tax with no exemptions whatsoever. He calls for a rate of 10% based on the Biblical tithe "because I think God is a pretty fair guy"*   Washington Post, "Someone Once Tried Ben Carson's Biblical Tax Plan," by Jim Tankersley, August 14, 2015, http:/www.washingtonpost.com/news/wonkblog/wp/2015/08/14/someone-once-tried-ben-carsons-biblical-tax-plan/, accessed October 1, 2015.

82   *former senator Rick Santorum is proposing a Flat Tax of 20%*   Wall Street Journal, "A Flat Tax Is the Best Path to Prosperity," by Rick Santorum, October 11, 2015, http://www.wsj.com/articles/a-flat-tax-is-the-best-path-to-prosperity-1444600639, accessed October 12, 2015.

83   *Rand Paul offers a variation of a Flat Tax that he calls the "The Fair and Flat Tax"*   Rand Paul for President, undated, https://www.randpaul.com/issue/taxes, accessed October 1, 2015.

83   *his proposed "business activity tax," a uniform 14.5% consumption tax on companies*   Ibid.

83   *"would be levied on revenues minus allowable expenses, such as the purchase of parts, computers and office equipment. All capital purchases would be immediately expensed, ending complicated depreciation schedules"*   Ibid.

83   *Dan Mitchell rightly points out that Paul's business activity tax is a version of the dreaded Value Added Tax (VAT)*   Forbes.com, "Senator Rand Paul's Very Good Tax Plan Needs One Important Tweak," by Daniel J. Mitchell, June 18, 2015, http://www.forbes.com/sites/danielmitchell/2015/06/18/senator-rand-pauls-very-good-tax-plan-needs-one-important-tweak/, accessed October 1, 2015.

83   *Mike Huckabee, however, is the most vigorous advocate of the Fair Tax*   Huckabee 2016, undated, http://www.mikehuckabee.com/abolishtheirs, accessed October 1, 2015.

84   *this scheme would place a 30% levy on all services and new products. It replaces personal and corporate income tax, payroll taxes, the death tax, and taxes on savings. . . . Two categories of transactions would be exempt*   FairTax.org, "Consumption Tax Should Replace Income Tax," by David Baron, May 28, 2015, https://fairtax.org/articles/consumption-tax-should-replace-income-tax, accessed October 1, 2015; FairTax.org, Frequently Asked Questions, https://fairtax.org/faq, accessed October 1, 2015.

84   *Fair Tax advocates advertise a 23% rate. In fact the real rate is 30%*   Ibid.

85   *more than 43% of American households paid no tax in 2013*   Tax Policy Center, "Who Doesn't Pay Federal Taxes?," undated, http://www.taxpolicycenter.org/taxtopics/federal-taxes-households.cfm, accessed October 1, 2015.

85   *each month, Washington would issue every household a check to offset the tax lev-*
ied on necessities   FairTax.org, "How FairTax works," undated, https://fairtax
.org/about/how-fairtax-works, accessed October 1, 2015.

85   *this is not an entitlement, but a rebate (in advance) of taxes paid—thus the term*
prebate. . . . For example, a two adult/two child family spending at the poverty level
has an 0% effective tax rate because the annual prebate of $7,328 refunds all of the
taxes they pay on their annual spending of $31,860   FairTax.org, "The FairTax
Prebate Explained," undated http://fairtax-psyclone.netdna-ssl.com/media/
attachments/549999512017a86464000320.pdf?1422935460, accessed October 1,
2015.

86   *13 million people live in poverty in America's cities*   The Brookings Institution,
"New Census Data Show Few Metro Areas Made Progress Against Poverty in
2013," by Elizabeth Kneebone and Natalie Holmes, September 19, 2014, http://
www.brookings.edu/research/reports/2014/09/19-census-metros-progress
-poverty-kneebone-holmes, accessed October 1, 2015.

86   *the cost of a prebate program has been estimated to be as high as $543 million*
"The FairTax Prebate Explained," op.cit.

86   *five states have no sales tax*   Tax Foundation, "State and Local Sales Tax Rates,
Midyear 2015," by Scott Drenkard and Jared Walczak, July 9, 2015, http://
taxfoundation.org/article/state-and-local-sales-tax-rates-midyear-2015,
accessed October 1, 2015.

86   *the states would do the job since most already have sales tax collection machinery*
FairTax.org, Frequently Asked Questions, op.cit.

86   *as an incentive, they would keep one-quarter of 1% of the fair tax revenues they*
gather   Ibid.

87   *New York's state and city taxes on cigarettes*   International Business Times,
"The Price Of Cigarettes: How Much Does a Pack Cost in Each US State?" by
Lisa Mahapatra, February 5, 2014, http://www.ibtimes.com/price-cigarettes
-how-much-does-pack-cost-each-us-state-map-1553445, accessed October 13,
2015.

88   *over half the cigarettes sold in New York City are bootlegs, imported from Native*
American reservations or low-tax states   Tax Foundation, "Cigarette Taxes and
Cigarette Smuggling by State, 2013," by Scott Drenkard, and Joseph Henchman,
February 6, 2015, http://taxfoundation.org/article/cigarette-taxes-and-cigarette
-smuggling-state-2013-0, accessed October 1, 2015.

88   *sellers will even create cigarette packages that have tax stamps that look like the real*
thing   New York Post, "Despite Law, Tribe Sells 1.7 Tons of Cigarettes Online,"
December 2, 2013, http://nypost.com/2013/12/02/despite-law-tribe-sells-1-7
-tons-of-cigarettes-online/, accessed October 1, 2015.

88   *Retailers, like the states, would get a quarter of 1% incentive to collect the*
tax   FairTax.org, Frequently Asked Questions, op.cit.

88   *there are nearly 10,000 sales tax jurisdictions in the United States*   Tax
Foundation, "State Sales Tax Jurisdictions Approach 10,000," by Joseph
Henchman and Richard Borean, March 24, 2014, http://taxfoundation.org/blog/
state-sales-tax-jurisdictions-approach-10000, accessed October 1, 2015.

88   *Washington politicians are already pushing legislation that would crush small*
e-commerce retailers   Forbes.com, "Congress Renews Push For Internet Sales
Tax . . . Will It Stick This Time?" by Joe Harpaz, March 24, 2015, http://www

.forbes.com/sites/joeharpaz/2015/03/24/congress-renews-push-for-internet
-sales-tax-will-it-stick-this-time/, accessed October 13, 2015.

88   *$7.9 billion in improper or fraudulent benefits in 2012*   Letter from Senator
      Charles Grassley to the Commissioner of the Social Security Administration,
      June   4,   2013,   http://www.grassley.senate.gov/sites/default/files/about/upload/
      2013-06-04-CEG-to-SSA-Improper-Payments.pdf, accessed October 1, 2015.

88   *the SSA's Old-Age, Survivors, and Disability Insurance payments alone accounted
      for $1.9 billion in erroneous payments in 2013*   Social Security Administration,
      "Annual Payment Recapture Audit Report," November 2014, http://www.ssa
      .gov/improperpayments/documents/Annual_PRA_Report_2014_10_30_14
      .pdf, accessed October 1, 2015.

88   *the tax agency issued 23,994 checks totaling $46,378,040 to a single address in
      Atlanta, Georgia in 2011*   U.S. Department of the Treasury, "Substantial
      Changes Are Needed to the Individual Taxpayer Identification Number Program
      to Detect Fraudulent Applications," July 16, 2012, https://www.treasury.gov/
      tigta/auditreports/2012reports/201242081fr.pdf, accessed October 1, 2015.

89   *according to one estimate, about 40% of state sales taxes fall improperly on business
      inputs*   Council on State Taxation, "What's Wrong with Taxing Business Services?,"
      by Robert Cline, Andrew Phillips and Tom Neubig, April 4, 2013, http://www
      .cost.org/workarea/downloadasset.aspx?id=83841, accessed October 1, 2015.

90   *a Fair Tax would require repeal of the 16th Amendment to the Constitution*
      FairTax.org, Frequently Asked Questions, op.cit.

90   *in 1895, the Supreme Court ruled that the Constitution doesn't give the federal gov-
      ernment the authority to enact an income tax. The subsequent 16th Amendment
      overruled that decision, granting Congress the "power to lay and collect taxes on
      incomes, from whatever source derived, without apportionment among the several
      States, and without regard to any census or enumeration"*   National Constitution
      Center, "16th Amendment: Income Tax," December 16, 2013, http://
      blog.constitutioncenter.org/2013/12/16th-amendment-income-tax/,   accessed
      October 1, 2015.

Chapter 8   Why Flat Tax Critics Are Flat Out Wrong

93   *compared with a measly $4,000 under the present system. Right now the standard
      deductions are $6,300 for an individual and $12,600 for a married couple*   Internal
      Revenue Service, "2015 Federal Tax Rates, Personal Exemptions, and Standard
      Deductions," by Elizabeth Rosen, September 30, 2015, http://www.irs.com/
      articles/2015-federal-tax-rates-personal-exemptions-and-standard-deductions,
      accessed September 30, 2015.

94   *they pay a higher percent of their income for tax preparation than higher earn-
      ing people—4.5%*   Tax Foundation, "The Cost of Complying with the Federal
      Income Tax," by J. Scott Moody, July 1, 2002, http://taxfoundation.org/article/
      cost-complying-federal-income-tax, accessed September 30, 2015.

95   *in 1981, the top 1% of American earners accounted for nearly 18% of federal per-
      sonal income tax revenue. By 1988, that same group accounted for nearly 28%,
      an increase of 10 percentage points in only 7 years*   Tax Foundation, "Summary
      of Latest Federal Income Tax Data," by Kyle Pomerleau, December 18, 2013,
      http://taxfoundation.org/article/summary-latest-federal-income-tax-data,
      accessed September 30, 2015.

95   *research from Stanford University . . . From 1995 to 2007, overall, a period of prosperity, charitable giving rose sharply*   The Russell Sage Foundation and The Stanford Center on Poverty and Inequality, "Charitable Giving and the Great Recession," by Rob Reich and Christopher Wimer, October 2012, https://web .stanford.edu/group/recessiontrends/cgi-bin/web/sites/all/themes/barron/pdf/ CharitableGiving_fact_sheet.pdf, accessed September 30, 2015.

95   *there was one notable decline*   Ibid.

96   *according to the Committee for a Responsible Federal Budget data, nearly $300 billion was donated to 1.1 million charities in 2011. But only $175 billion of that was deducted as a charitable contribution*   Committee for a Responsible Federal Budget, "The Tax Break-Down: Charitable Deduction," December 16, 2013, http://crfb.org/blogs/tax-break-down-charitable-deduction, accessed September 30, 2015.

96   *"Ice Bucket Challenge," that raised awareness and research funding for Lou Gehrig's disease, which generated $115 million for the ALS Association in a six-week period in 2014*   ALS Association, "ALS Ice Bucket Challenge—FAQ," undated, http:// www.alsa.org/about-us/ice-bucket-challenge-faq.html, accessed September 27, 2015.

96   *Americans' cash contributions to charities have always been roughly 2% of GDP. In hard times it might fall to 1.8% and when the economy is booming it might rise to 2.2%*   The Russell Sage Foundation and The Stanford Center on Poverty and Inequality, op. cit.

96   *in the last 35 years, Congress has substantially altered the tax code several times—1981, 1986, and 2003. The changes involved substantial cuts in individual rates*   Tax Foundation, "Federal Individual Income Tax Rates History: Income Years 1913–2013," undated, http://taxfoundation.org/sites/taxfoundation.org/ files/docs/fed_individual_rate_history_adjusted.pdf, accessed September 30, 2015.

96   *in 2001, Congress passed legislation to phase out the Death Tax*   Tax Foundation, "The Federal Estate Tax: Will it Rise From the Grave in 2011 or Sooner?," by William Ahern, May 2010, http://taxfoundation.org/sites/taxfoundation.org/ files/docs/sr179.pdf, accessed September 30, 2015.

96   *the 1980s: When the top personal rate was slashed from 70% to 28%*   Tax Foundation, "Federal Individual Income Tax Rates History," op. cit.

97   *from 1980 to 1989, individual donations grew at an annual rate of 5.2%*   Hoover Institution, "Hoover Classics: Flat Tax," undated, http://www.hoover.org/sites/ default/files/uploads/documents/0817993115_157.pdf, accessed September 30, 2015.

97   *in 1988, Senator Robert Packwood*   Heritage Foundation, "The Correct Way to Measure the Revenue Impact of Changes in Tax Rates," by Daniel J. Mitchell, May 3, 2002, http://www.heritage.org/research/reports/2002/05/correct-way-to -measure-the-revenue-impact-of-changes-in-tax-rates, accessed September 29, 2015.

98   *Federal collections fell from about $53 billion*   Tax Foundation, "Federal Capital Gains Tax Collections," 1954–2009, http://taxfoundation.org/article/ federal-capital-gains-tax-collections-1954-2009, accessed October 25, 2015.

98   *the CBO predicted that the 1986 increase in the capital gains levy would raise more revenue*   National Center for Policy Analysis, "Tax Briefing Book," edited

by Joe Barnett, http://www.ncpa.org/pdfs/TAXBriefingBook-97.pdf, accessed September 29, 2015.

99   *President George W. Bush's 2003 capital gains tax cut*   Tax Policy Center, "The Bush Tax Cuts: How Did the 2003 Tax Cuts Change the Tax Code?," by William Gale and Benjamin Harris, updated January 23, 2008, http://www.taxpolicy center.org/briefing-book/background/bush-tax-cuts/2003.cfm, accessed September 29, 2015.

99   *unemployment immediately began to drop from around 6% to 4.4% in 2006 before the financial crisis*   Bureau of Labor Statistics Data Tools, http://data.bls.gov/timeseries/LNS14000000, accessed September 26, 2015.

100   *the Flat Tax would lower interest rates by about 20% in a normal interest rate environment*   Robert E. Hall, Alvin Rabushka, Dick Armey, Robert Eisner, and Herbert Stein, *Fairness and Efficiency in the Flat Tax* (The AEI Press, 1996), p. 35, http://www.aei.org/wp-content/uploads/2011/10/20040218_book338.pdf, accessed September 29, 2015.

100   *economists and Flat Tax architects Robert Hall and Alvin Rabushka, who did their groundbreaking work at Stanford University's Hoover Institution, have explained that*   Ibid.

102   *Reagan slashed the top federal rate to 28% in 1986*   American Enterprise Institute, "The Tax Reform Evidence from 1986," by Martin Feldstein, October 24, 2011, https://www.aei.org/publication/the-tax-reform-evidence-from-1986/, accessed September 29, 2015.

102   *several states, including New York, reduced their rates*   Center on Budget and Policy Priorities, "State Personal Income Tax Cuts: Still a Poor Strategy for Economic Growth," by Michael Leachman and Michael Mazerov, May 14, 2015, http://www.cbpp.org/research/state-budget-and-tax/state-personal-income -tax-cuts-still-a-poor-strategy-for-economic, accessed September 30, 2015.

Chapter 9 Why Our Current System of Unstable Money Has Been a Critical Part of the Problem

107   *the weakening of the yuan sent the Dow Jones Average down more than 1,000 points*   Barron's, "Dow Drops More Than 1,000 Points," by Vito J. Racanelli, August 22, 2015, http://www.barrons.com/articles/dow-drops-more-than-1-000 -points-1440224896, accessed October 14, 2015.

107   *closing out the third quarter with significant losses*   MarketWatch.com, "Dow Suffers Rare 3-Quarter Losing Streak," by Tomi Kilgore, September 30, 2015, http://www.marketwatch.com/story/dow-to-suffer-rare-3-quarter-losing-streak-2015-09-30, accessed October 14, 2015.

108   *there have been currency crises in Russia, Turkey, and South Africa*   The *Financial Times*, "Emerging Markets Grapple With Rouble Crisis," by Jonathan Wheatley, December 16, 2014, http://www.ft.com/cms/s/0/2ba83ad8-8517 -11e4-bb63-00144feabdc0.html#axzz3oaOJP7t4, accessed October 14, 2015. Mohammed Aly Sergie, "Currency Crises in Emerging Markets, Council on Foreign Relations Backgrounder, January 24, 2014, http://www.cfr.org/emerging -markets/currency-crises-emerging-markets/p31843, accessed October 14, 2015.

108   *even the once-impressive Australian dollar has been clobbered*   Business Insider, "Australian Dollar Gets Clobbered," by Joe Weisenthal, January 16, 2014, http://www.businessinsider.com/aussie-dollar-falls-2014-1, accessed October 14, 2015.

108 *Brazil . . . economy slid into recession*   *CNNMoney*, "Brazil Falls Deep Into Recession," by Patrick Gillespie, August 28, 2015, http://money.cnn.com/2015/08/28/news/economy/brazil-recession/, accessed October 14, 2015.

108 *for most of our history, the U.S. relied on sound money. The dollar was pegged to gold and had a fixed value*   Library of Economics and Liberty, "Gold Standard," by Michael D. Bordo, http://www.econlib.org/library/Enc/GoldStandard.html, accessed October 14, 2015.

108 *then in 1971 Richard Nixon severed the link to gold*   Ibid.

108 *a study by noted economists from Rutgers University, the University of California at Berkeley and the World Bank*   Michael Bordo, Barry Eichengreen, Daniela Klingebiel, Maria Soledad Martinez-Peria and Andrew K. Rose, "Is the Crisis Problem Growing More Severe?" *Economic Policy*, 32:51–82.

111 *according to the government's Consumer Price Index Inflation Calculator, the dollar's buying power has decreased by 28% since the dollar started weakening fifteen years ago. A dollar in 2015 buys what .72 cents did in 2000*   Bureau of Labor Statistics, U.S. Department of Labor, Consumer Prince Index Inflation Calculator, available at http://www.bls.gov/data/inflation_calculator.htm, accessed October 14, 2015.

111 *a stealth tax whereby "government can confiscate, secretly and unobserved, an important part of the wealth of their citizens"*   John Maynard Keynes, *The Economic Consequences of the Peace* (Keynes Press, 2013), p. 138.

111 *"history is replete with Great Disorders in which social cohesion has been undermined by currency debasements"*   Dylan Grice, "The Loss of Trust and the Great Disorder," *Edelweiss Journal*, no. 9, October 2012, p. 1, http://www.edelweissjournal.com/pdfs/EdelweissJournal-009.pdf, accessed October 14, 2015.

112 *is summed up best by John Locke*   John Locke, *The Works of John Locke: Vol. 5* (London: Thomas Davison, Whitefriars, 1823), p. 144

112 *monetary instability correlates with increases in criminal activity*   John M. Nunley, Richard Alan Seals Jr., and Joachim Zietz, "The Impact of Macroeconomic Conditions on Property Crime," Auburn Economics Working Paper (Auburn University, 2011), p. 18, http://cla.auburn.edu/econwp/Archives/2011/2011-06.pdf, accessed October 14, 2015; Chor Foon Tang and Hooi Hooi Lean, "Will Inflation Increase Crime Rate? New Evidence from Bounds and Modified Wald Tests," *Global Crime* 8(4), November 2007, pp. 311–323, http://www.tandfonline.com/doi/full/10.1080/17440570701739694 (abstract), accessed October 14, 2015.

112 *Henry Hazlitt observed the relationship between crime and loose money*   Henry Hazlitt, "Inflation vs. Immorality," Freeman, January 1, 1977, http://fee.org/freeman/inflation-vs-immorality/, accessed October 14, 2015.

114 *Germany, for one, responded*   Matthew Karnitschnig, "Germany's Expensive Gamble on Renewable Energy," *Wall Street Journal*, August 26, 2014, http://www.wsj.com/articles/germanys-expensive-gamble-on-renewable-energy-1409106602, accessed October 14, 2015.

114 *demand, for example, cannot account for oil plunging to as low as $10 a barrel in 1999 or, in the early 2000s, rocketing from $25 to over $100 a barrel*   U.S. Energy Information Administration, U.S. Department of Energy, U.S. Crude Oil First Purchase Price, available at http://www.eia.gov/dnav/pet/hist/LeafHandler.ashx?n=PET&s=F000000__3&f=M, accessed October 14, 2015.

115 *also playing a key role were the reinstatement of mark-to-market account-ing rules* Forbes.com, "Suspend Mark-to-Market Now!" by Newt Gingrich, September 29, 2008, http://www.forbes.com/2008/09/29/mark-to-market-oped -cx_ng_0929gingrich.html.

115 *the stage for this disaster was set in 2001* Wall Street Journal, "The Dangers of an Interventionist Fed," by John Taylor, March 29. 2012, http://www.wsj.com/ articles/SB10001424052702303816504577307403971824094, accessed October 14, 2015.

115 *the government-sponsored enterprises (GSEs) Fannie Mae and then Freddie Mac* USA Today, "Fannie, Freddie Caused the Financial Crisis," by Peter J. Wallison, November 25, 2011, http://www.aei.org/article/economics/financial-services/housing-finance/fannie-freddie-caused-the-financial-crisis/, accessed October 14, 2015.

116 *the Fed added some $3.5 trillion to its balance sheet through bond purchases. This growth in bank reserves was proportionately twice what occurred in the 1970s. This was about equal to the size of the German economy* Bloomberg.com, "The Fed Eases Off," by Jeff Kearns, September 16, 2015, http://www.bloombergview.com/ quicktake/federal-reserve-quantitative-easing-tape, accessed October 14, 2015.

Chapter 10 What's Wrong with the Federal Reserve and Why It Can't Guide the Economy

119 *Fed Chairman Ben Bernanke was named "Person of the Year 2009" by Time* Time, "Person of the Year: Ben Bernanke," by Michael Grunewald, December 16, 2009, http://content.time.com/time/specials/packages/article/ 0,28804,1946375_1947251_1947520,00.html, accessed October 14, 2015.

120 *thanks to the Dodd-Frank bill* Cato Institute, "Dodd-Frank's Expansion of Fed Power: A Historical Perspective," by Norbert Michel, *Cato Journal* 16(3), Fall 2014, pp. 557–567, http://object.cato.org/sites/cato.org/files/serials/files/ cato-journal/2014/9/cj34n3-6.pdf, accessed October 14, 2015.

120 *the Federal Reserve is comprised of twelve regional banks around the coun-try* Board of Governors of the Federal Reserve System, "The Structure of the Federal Reserve System," http://www.federalreserve.gov/pubs/frseries/frseri.htm, accessed October 14, 2015.

120 *by setting interest rates, primarily through "open market operations"—the buying or selling of Treasury securities . . . to increase or reduce the monetary base* Board of Governors of the Federal Reserve System, "Credit and Liquidity Programs and the Balance Sheet," http://www.federalreserve.gov/monetarypolicy/bst_ openmarketops.htm, accessed October 14, 2015.

121 *instead, it helped produce the weakest ever rebound from a major downturn* Pew Research Center, "Five years In, Recovery Still Underwhelms Compared with Previous Ones," by Drew DeSilver, June 23, 2014, http://www.pewresearch .org/fact-tank/2014/06/23/five-years-in-recovery-still-underwhelms-compared -with-previous-ones/, accessed October 14, 2015.

121 *with annual growth rates stuck at around 2%* Center on Budget and Policy Priorities, "Chart Book: The Legacy of the Great Recession," http://www.cbpp .org/research/economy/chart-book-the-legacy-of-the-great-recession, accessed October 14, 2015.

121 *has amassed a portfolio of bonds and mortgages exceeding $3 trillion with money created out of thin air* TheBlaze.com, "Quantitative Easing Is Over, For Now. Take a Look at How Many Trillions of Dollars It Cost," by Zach Noble, October 29, 2014, http://www.theblaze.com/stories/2014/10/29/quantitative-easing -is-over-for-now-take-a-look-at-how-many-trillions-of-dollars-it-cost/, accessed October 14, 2015.

121 *but the low-interest loans made under this program went primarily to large corporations and to the government itself* McKinsey Global Institute, "QE and Ultra-Low Interest Rates: Distributional Effects and Risks," by Richard Dobbs, Susan Lund, Tim Koller and Ari Shwayder, November 2013, http://www mckinsey.com/insights/economic_studies/qe_and_ultra_low_interest_rates_ distributional_effects_and_risks, accessed October 14, 2015.

121 *in contrast, Operation Twist focused on lowering long-term interest rates* Forbes .com, "Investors Face a Cruel Backlash from Ben Bernanke's Operation Twist," by Barry Poulson, December 19, 2012, www.forbes.com/sites/realspin/2012/12/19/ investors-face-a-cruel-backlash-from-ben-bernankes-operation-twist/, accessed October 14, 2015.

121 *meanwhile, large corporations borrowed more* "QE and Ultra-Low Interest Rates: Distributional Effects and Risks," Op cit.

122 *Apple, which has a staggering cash hoard of $200 billion, has issued some $40 billion of bonds* BloombergView.com, "Apple Bonds and Endless Mortgage Suits," by Matt Levine, June 5, 2015, http://www.bloombergview.com/articles/2015-06-05/ apple-bonds-and-endless-mortgage-suits, accessed October 14, 2015.

122 *the Fed indirectly helped to revive them, thanks to fees they received from the sales of mortgage-backed securities* Forbes.com, "Fannie Mae and Freddie Mac Profits: A Creative Accounting Technique," by Richard Lehmann, August 12, 2013, http://www.forbes.com/sites/investor/2013/08/12/fannie-mae-and-freddie -mac-profits-a-creative-accounting-technique/, accessed October 14, 2015.

122 *most of the QE liquidity never made it into the economy* Huffington Post, "Massive Misconceptions about Where the Bernanke Fed's Money Explosion Went," by Robert Auerbach, June 25, 2013, http://www.huffingtonpost .com/robert-auerbach/massive-misconceptions-ab_b_3490373.html, accessed October 14, 2015.

122 *the Fed's massive purchases of long-term Treasury bonds have created a shortage for insurers and pension funds* "QE and Ultra-Low Interest Rates: Distributional Effects and Risks," Op.cit.

123 *also hurt have been individual savers, especially the elderly* TheEconomist .com, "QE Was Not About Saving the Banks," by Buttonwood, September 28, 2015, http://www.economist.com/blogs/buttonwood/2015/09/monetary-policy -and-economics, accessed October 14, 2015.

123 *among them was noted economist Steve Moore* Washington Times, "Why I Can't Get a Mortgage," by Steve Moore, August 23, 2015, www.washington times.com/news/2015/aug/23/stephen-moore-mortgage-woes-of-the-middle -class/, accessed October 14, 2015.

123 *"here we are with the lowest interest rates in 50 years"* Ibid.

123 *Uncle Sam is repeating every mistake it made just eight years ago* Ibid.

124 *Federal Reserve Board Chair Janet Yellen's stated desire to generate an inflation rate of 2%* BusinessInsider.com, "Janet Yellen's First FOMC Press Conference," by

Matthew Boesler, March 19, 2015, http://www.businessinsider.com/march-fomc
-press-conference-2014-3, accessed October 14, 2015.

124 *disproven by seven Nobel Prize–winning economists and numerous others, the*
Phillips Curve   Forbes.com, "Nobel after Nobel Won't Kill the Phillips Curve,"
by Brian Domitrovic, March 7, 2011, http://www.forbes.com/sites/brian
domitrovic/2011/03/07/nobel-after-nobel-wont-kill-the-phillips-curve/,
accessed October 14, 2015.

124 *economic historian Brian Domitrovic has pointed out on Forbes.com*   Forbes
.com, "When It Comes to Job Creation, Obama Doesn't Hold a Candle to
Reagan," by Brian Domitrovic, October 9, 2012, http://www.forbes.com/sites/
briandomitrovic/2012/10/09/when-it-comes-to-job-creation-obama-doesnt
-hold-a-candle-to-reagan/, accessed October 14, 2015.

125 *in his book,* Knowledge and Power, *George Gilder*   Knowledge and Power:
The Information Theory of Capitalism and How It Is Revolutionizing Our World
George Gilder (Washington, DC: Regnery Publishing, 2013), pp. 1–6.

126 *the Fed inadvertently created an artificial shortage of dollars that sent commod-*
ity prices plunging   Zerohedge.com, "The 'Deflationary Vortex': Global Dollar
Economy Suffers Biggest Plunge Since Lehman, Down $4 Trillion," by Tyler Durden,
http://www.zerohedge.com/news/2015-01-20/deflationary-vortex-global
-dollar-economy-suffers-biggest-plunge-lehman-down-4-trill, accessed October
25, 2015.

126 *the economies of major commodity-producing countries such as Brazil, South*
Africa, Indonesia, and Russia have been sent into a tailspin   Reuters, "Global
Commodity Price Slump Sends Ripples Around the World," by Matthew Mpoke
Bigg, October 3, 2015, http://fortune.com/2015/10/03/global-commodity
-price-slump-economic-fallout/, accessed October 25, 2015.

127 *this has heaped crushing costs on smaller banks*   RealClearMarkets.com, "Basel
III Hurts Community Banks and Consumers," by Victor Nava, November
1, 2012, http://www.realclearmarkets.com/articles/2012/11/01/basel_iii_hurts_
community_banks_and_consumers_99966.html, accessed October 14, 2015.

128 *one insurer, MetLife, is courageously fighting its FISI designation*   New York
Times, "MetLife Sues Over Being Named Too Big to Fail," by Mary Williams
Walsh, January 13, 2015, http://dealbook.nytimes.com/2015/01/13/metlife-to
-fight-too-big-to-fail-status-in-court/, accessed October 14, 2015.

128 *the CFPB is waging a jihad against auto dealers*   AmericanBanker.com, "Car
Dealers Fight Back Against CFPB Auto Financing Rule," by Rachel Witkowski,
March 22, 2013, http://www.americanbanker.com/issues/178_57/car-dealers
-fight-back-against-cfpb-auto-financing-rule-1057779-1.html, accessed October
14, 2015.

128 *another CFPB overreach: demanding the monthly card statements of almost*
every American   Watchdog.org, "Shadowy Federal Agency Snooping in Your
Wallet Accused of Discrimination," by M.D. Kittle, July 3, 2015, http://watchdog
.org/227457/federal-discrimination-cfpb/, accessed October 14, 2015.

Chapter 11 The Best Way to Stable Money Is the Gold Standard

133 *Roy Jastram observed in his classic work* The Golden Constant, *"The ring worn*
today may contain particles mined in the time of the Pharaohs"   *The Golden*
Constant, by Roy W. Jastram (New York: John Wiley & Sons, 1977), p. 189.

133 *price increases averaging under 2% a year*   Forbes.com, "Three Things About the Gold Standard That Everyone Should Know," by Nathan Lewis, August 21, 2015, http://www.forbes.com/sites/nathanlewis/2015/08/21/three-things-about-the-gold-standard-that-everyone-should-know/, accessed October 25, 2015.

134 *the resulting inflation was minimal and quickly receded*   California.gov, "The Discovery of Gold In California," by Donald C. Cutter, http://www.conservation.ca.gov/cgs/geologic_resources/gold/CA_GoldDiscovery_files, accessed October 14, 2015.

134 *Sir Isaac Newton, tied the pound to gold in 1717 at the rate of 3.89 pounds per ounce, a ratio that lasted more than two centuries*   GoldAvenue.com, "18th Century," http://info.goldavenue.com/info_site/in_arts/in_mill/18thcentury.htm, accessed September 24, 2015.

135 *he fixed the dollar by law to a specific weight of gold—$19.39 per ounce. (There was a slight devaluation in 1834 to $20.67 an ounce)*   Forbes.com, " Linking the Dollar to Gold," by Peter Ferrara, June 21, 2014, http://www.forbes.com/sites/peterferrara/2014/06/21/linking-the-dollar-to-gold-completing-the-recipe-for-restoring-an-economic-boom-for-america/, accessed September 24, 2015.

136 *after the war, Germany's money supply was five times the level it had been in the late 1930s. . . . and began slashing taxes*   The Library of Economics and Liberty, "German Economic Miracle," by David R. Henderson, undated, http://www.econlib.org/library/Enc/GermanEconomicMiracle.html, accessed September 24, 2015.

137 *"interest rates worldwide converged to low levels"*   Gold: the Monetary Polaris, by Nathan Lewis (Canyon Maple Publishing, 2013), p. 113, http://csinvesting.org/wp-content/uploads/2014/03/Gold-the-Monetary-Polaris.pdf, accessed September 24, 2015.

137 *yields on French government debt, for example, were at a catastrophic 15% when the Bank of France was established in 1800*   Ibid.

138 *in 1971, Arthur Burns, then Chairman of the Fed, went along with the plan*   Journal of Economic Perspectives, "How Richard Nixon Pressured Arthur Burns: Evidence from the Nixon Tapes," by Burton A. Abrams, Volume 20, Number 4, pgs. 177–188, http://nowandfutures.com/d3/Nixons_Fed_control_Abrams_jep-v20n42006.pdf, accessed September 24, 2015.

138 *"government can still borrow . . . government debt would have never gotten out of hand like it has"*   TheGoldStandardNow.org, "The Gold Standard: Power to the People," by Daniel M. Ryan, April 16th, 2011, http://www.thegoldstandardnow.org/daniel-m-ryan-62?start=5, accessed September 24, 2015.

Chatper 12 How a Gold Standard Would Work

141 *"the most perfect monetary system humans have yet created"*   Forbes.com, "The 1870–1914 Gold Standard: The Most Perfect One Ever Created," by Nathan Lewis, January 3, 2013, http://www.forbes.com/sites/nathanlewis/2013/01/03/the-1870-1914-gold-standard-the-most-perfect-one-ever-created/, accessed January 24, 2015.

142 *gold bullion reserve coverage in the United States in 1910 was 42% of banknotes in circulation. This coverage ratio varied in different countries*   Ibid.

143 *World War I*   Library of Economics and Liberty, "Gold Standard," by Michael D. Bordo, http://www.econlib.org/library/Enc/GoldStandard.html, accessed October 14, 2015.

143 *the gold exchange standard was the system implemented after both World Wars*   Cato Institute, "The Rise and Fall of the Gold Standard in the United States," by George Selgin, Policy Analysis No. 729, p. 13, June 20, 2013, http://object.cato.org/sites/cato.org/files/pubs/pdf/pa729_web.pdf, accessed October 14, 2015.

144 *guardians of the system—Britain after WWI and the U.S. after WWII—were unwilling to abide by its discipline*   TheGoldStandardNow.org, "Myth 7: The Gold Standard Was Responsible for the Deflation that Ushered in the Great Depression," by Lawrence H. White, December 10, 2012, http://www.thegoldstandardnow.org/the-lehrman-gold-standard-articles/1766-myth-7-the-gold-standard-was-responsible-for-the-deflation-that-ushered-in-the-great-depression, accessed October 14, 2015.

144 *U.S. Representative Ted Poe of Texas several years ago*   Mises Daily, "A Substandard Golden Rule," by Joseph T. Salerno, May 29, 2013, https://mises.org/library/substandard-golden-rule, accessed September 24, 2015.

145 *they equate partial coverage with our modern system of "fractional reserve banking"*   Mises Institute, "The Case for a 100% Gold Backed Dollar," by Murray N. Rothbard, p. 44, (free download) https://mises.org/library/case-100-percent-gold-dollar-2, accessed October 14, 2015.

145 *they believe that any gold standard should require a government possess enough gold to support a country's entire money stock*   p.19 op.cit.

146 *the global gold supply grows at about 2% a year*   JM Bullion, "Gold Supply," http://www.jmbullion.com/investing-guide/james/gold-supply/, accessed October 14, 2015.

146 *the current U.S. monetary base is around $4 trillion*   Federal Reserve Bank of St. Louis, "St. Louis Adjusted Monetary Base" (interactive chart) 10/08/2015, https://research.stlouisfed.org/fred2/series/BASE, accessed October 14, 2015.

146 *before Quantitative Easing, it was a little under $900 billion*   Ibid.

146 *Franklin Roosevelt did that in 1934 when he jacked up the dollar price of gold from $20.67 to $35.*   Wikipedia.org, "Gold Reserve Act," https://en.wikipedia.org/wiki/Gold_Reserve_Act, accessed September 24, 2015.

146 *currency boards have been around*   The Princeton Encyclopedia of the World Economy, "Currency Board Arrangement," by Kenneth A. Reinert, Ramkishen S. Rajan, Amy Joycelyn Glass, Lewis S. Davis (Princeton University Press, August 2, 2010), p. 240, https://books.google.com/books?id=YbDtAQAAQBAJ&pg=PA241&lpg=PA241&dq=currency+boards+have+been+around+150+years&source=bl&ots=GPk2-CeHWV&sig=uxxmQYSp5ogzRT8EFVb251hNOvI&hl=en&sa=X&ved=0CCYQ6AEwAWoVChMIxJa16s_CyAIVyn2QCh2wKguA#v=onepage&q=currency%20boards%20have%20been%20around%20150%20years&f=false, accessed October 14, 2015.

147 *"hold reserves in gold or in highly rated or liquid securities*   Cato Institute, "A Gold-Based Currency Board, Please," by Steve H. Hanke, http://www.cato.org/publications/commentary/goldbased-currency-board-please, accessed September 24, 2015.

149 *various taxes and fees on the sale of gold and silver, as well as capital gains taxes* CoinNews.net, "Ron Paul's Free Competition in Currency Act Reintroduced," by Mike Unser, January 7, 2013, http://www.coinnews.net/2013/01/07/ron-pauls-free-competition-in-currency-act-reintroduced/, accessed October 14, 2015.

149 *total supply is 261 million ounces today* Bureau of the Fiscal Service, "Status Report of U.S. Government Gold Reserve," August 31, 2015, https://www.fiscal.treasury.gov/fsreports/rpt/goldRpt/current_report.htm, accessed September 24, 2015.

Chapter 13 Debunking the Gold Myths

152 *economist Barry Eichengreen typifies this thinking when he writes that "gold's inherent price volatility" makes it unable to "provide a basis for international commercial and financial transactions on a twenty-first century scale"* Policy Analysis, "Recent Arguments against the Gold Standard," by Lawrence H. White, Cato Institute, June 20, 2013, http://object.cato.org/sites/cato.org/files/pubs/pdf/pa728_web.pdf, accessed October 14, 2015.

152 *liberal columnist Ezra Klein insists that, "The problems with the gold standard are legion"* Washington Post, "The GOP Has Picked the Wrong Time to Rediscover Gold," by Ezra Klein, August 24, 2012, http://www.washingtonpost.com/blogs/ezra-klein/wp/2012/08/24/the-gop-has-picked-the-wrong-time-to-rediscover-gold/, accessed October 14, 2015.

152 *in 2011, gold shot to a record high of $1,900* CNN Money, "Gold Tops $1900, Looking 'a Bit Bubbly,'" by Hibah Yousuf, August 23, 2011, http://money.cnn.com/2011/08/22/markets/gold_prices/, accessed October 14, 2015.

153 *retreating to around $1,100 an ounce in late 2015* MarketWatch.com, "Gold Ends Near $1,100 as Prices Rebound, Dollar Slides," by Myra P. Saefong and Sara Sjolin, July 27, 2015 http://www.marketwatch.com/story/gold-retakes-1100-as-dollar-slides-2015-07-27, accessed October 14, 2015.

153 *emotions calmed, the dollar price fell to $300 an ounce* The End of Prosperity: How Higher Taxes Will Doom the Economy—If We Let It Happen, by Arthur B. Laffer, Stephen Moore, Peter Tanous (New York: Simon & Schuster, 2008), p. 101.

153 *gold prices fluctuated between $325 and $440 an ounce through the Reagan era and into the 1990s, a period known as the "Great Moderation"* Federal Reserve Bank of St. Louis, "Gold Fixing Price 10:30 A.M. (London Time) in London Bullion Market, Based in U.S. Dollars," https://research.stlouisfed.org/fred2/series/GOLDAMGBD228NLBM#, accessed October 14, 2015.

153 *United States has only about 261 million ounces of gold* Bureau of the Fiscal Service, U.S. Department of the Treasury, "Status Report of U.S. Government Gold Reserve," https://www.fiscal.treasury.gov/fsreports/rpt/goldRpt/current_report.htm, accessed October 14, 2015.

153 *the monetary base is over $4 trillion* Federal Reserve Bank of St. Louis, "St. Louis Adjusted Monetary Base," https://research.stlouisfed.org/fred2/series/BASE/, accessed October 14, 2015.

153 *and the most commonly used money supply measure, M2, stands at over $12 trillion* Federal Reserve Bank of St. Louis, "M2 Money Stock," https://research.stlouisfed.org/fred2/series/M2, accessed October 14, 2015.

154 *no country ever had 100% gold backing for its money*   Forbes.com, "The 1870–1914 Gold Standard: The Most Perfect One Ever Created," by Nathan Lewis, January 3, 2013, http://www.forbes.com/sites/nathanlewis/2013/01/03/the-1870-1914-gold-standard-the-most-perfect-one-ever-created/, accessed October 14, 2015.

154 *the ratio in the U.S. was around 42% in the early 1900s and had been lower before then*   Ibid.

154 *Great Britain also had very low amounts of gold backing the pound*   Ibid.

154 *Bernanke expressed this concern in a college lecture, "Because the money supply is determined by the supply of gold, it cannot be adjusted in response to changing economic conditions"*   Policy Analysis, "Recent Arguments against the Gold Standard," by Lawrence H. White, vol. 728, p. 10, http://object.cato.org/sites/cato.org/files/pubs/pdf/pa728_web.pdf, accessed October 14, 2015.

154 *Larry White explains that Bernanke's warning is a fallacy*   Ibid. p. 11.

155 *a lesson from history: the U.S. money supply exploded between 1775 and 1900*   Forbes.com, "The Gold Standard and the Myth About Money Growth," by Nathan Lewis, February 16, 2012, http://www.forbes.com/sites/nathanlewis/2012/02/16/the-gold-standard-and-the-myth-about-money-growth/.

155 *the model of "lender of last resort" was developed by the Bank of England*   RichmondFed.org "Lender of Last Resort: The Concept in History," by Thomas M. Humphrey, 1989, https://www.richmondfed.org/~/media/richmondfedorg/publications/research/economic_review/1989/pdf/er750202.pdf, accessed October 14, 2015.

156 *the Great Depression was a disastrous consequence of the global trade war ignited by America's enactment of the Smoot-Hawley Tariff Act*   Forbes.com, "Was the Gold Standard the Cause of the Great Depression?" by Nathan Lewis, April 1, 2012, http://www.forbes.com/sites/nathanlewis/2012/04/01/was-the-gold-standard-the-cause-of-the-great-depression/, accessed October 14, 2015.

156 *the stock market crashed when it appeared that Smoot-Hawley would likely pass Congress*   National Review, "What Do We Know about the Great Crash?" by Alan Reynolds, September 9, 1979, p. 1418, http://object.cato.org/sites/cato.org/files/articles/reynolds_speech_19791109.pdf, accessed October 14, 2015.

156 *policy makers—in the U.S and around the world—didn't understand what was happening*   Gold: The Once and Future Money, by Nathan Lewis (Hoboken, NJ: John Wiley & Sons, 2007), pp. 211–238.

156 *United States, for example, in 1932 passed a bill of astonishing tax hikes. Income tax rates were raised exponentially, with the top rate more than doubling, to 63%*   Forbes.com, "Was the Gold Standard the Cause of the Great Depression?" by Nathan Lewis, April 1, 2012, http://www.forbes.com/sites/nathanlewis/2012/04/01/was-the-gold-standard-the-cause-of-the-great-depression/.

156 *a stamp tax on checks accelerated the economy's downward spiral*   Forbes.com, "Fifteen Minutes of Pain," by Amity Shlaes, May 1, 2009, http://www.forbes.com/2009/04/30/1930s-great-depression-business-shlaes.html.

156 *increases of excise taxes on items such as candy and movie tickets*   Cato Institute, "How FDR's New Deal Harmed Millions of Poor People," by Jim Powell, December 29, 2003, http://www.cato.org/publications/commentary/how-fdrs-new-deal-harmed-millions-poor-people.

156 *things were nearly as bad in Great Britain, which raised income taxes in 1930 and again in 1931. The Germans were especially hard hit by the trade war and*

responded with a battery of taxes that deepened the slump Gold: The Once and Future Money, by Nathan Lewis (Hoboken, NJ: John Wiley & Sons, 2007), pp. 211–238.

157 *floundering and confused, many governments then turned to debasing their money by going off the gold standard, led by Great Britain in late 1931* Ibid.

157 *after London's devaluation, at least 20 countries quickly followed suit. The United States did the same in 1934, as did Italy and Belgium; France finally devalued the franc in 1936* Ibid.

157 *"it was due to many countries leaving the gold standard, inflating massively while off the gold standard, and then resuming the gold standard at the old parity (not devaluing to accommodate a higher price level)"* TheGoldStandardNow.org, "Myth 7: The Gold Standard Was Responsible for the Deflation that Ushered in the Great Depression," by Lawrence H. White, December 10, 2012, http://www.thegoldstandardnow.org/the-lehrman-gold-standard-articles/1766-myth-7-the-gold-standard-was-responsible-for-the-deflation-that-ushered-in-the-great-depression, accessed October 14, 2015.

158 *Soros and others ultimately pocketed billions in profits* Forbes.com, "How George Soros Broke the British Pound and Why Hedge Funds Probably Can't Crack the Euro," by Steve Schaefer, July 7, 2015, http://www.forbes.com/sites/steveschaefer/2015/07/07/forbes-flashback-george-soros-british-pound-euro-ecb/.

158 *in 2009, Russia thwarted an attack on the ruble by buying its own currency* Forbes.com, "Russia's Currency Crisis: This Is So 2008," by Nathan Lewis, October 16, 2014, http://www.forbes.com/sites/nathanlewis/2014/10/16/russias-currency-crisis-this-is-so-2008/.

159 *combined with the realistic franc/gold ratio, France prospered and avoided Britain's economic travails of that era* Gold: The Once and Future Money, Nathan Lewis (Hoboken, NJ: John Wiley & Sons, 2007), pp. 211–238.

Chapter 14 Bring Back America

163 *health savings accounts (HSAs) are IRA-like accounts that enable you to set aside tax-free dollars to pay for healthcare. Under current law, you and your employer are permitted to make tax-free contributions to your HSA. But the amounts of permissible contributions are limited* Internal Revenue Service, "Publication 969," undated, https://www.irs.gov/publications/p969/ar02.html#en_US_2014_publink1000204020, accessed October 13, 2015.

164 *requiring more than 80,000 agents for tax collection and enforcement* Internal Revenue Service, "Personnel Summary, by Employment Status, Budget Activity, and Selected Type of Personnel," updated March 24, 2015, accessed October 13, 2015.

164 *the Federal Reserve System was founded more than a century ago* Federal Reserve, "History of the Federal Reseve," undated, https://www.federalreserveeducation.org/about-the-fed/history, accessed October 13, 2015.

164 *the Nixon Administration in 1971 severed the dollar's link to gold* Gold: The Once and Future Money, Nathan Lewis (Hoboken, NJ: John Wiley & Sons, 2007), p. 15.

165 *gold standard, which served this country well for 180 years, from the time of George Washington's presidency to the early 1970s* Lewis, op. cit., p. 155.

If You Want To Learn More: Recommended Reading

Domitrivic, Brian. *Econoclasts: The Rebels who Sparked the Supply-Side Revolution and Restored American Prosperity.* Intercollegiate Studies Institute.

Gilder, George. *Knowledge and Power.* Regnery Publishing.

Gilder, George. *The Twenty-first Century Case for Gold: A New Information Theory of Money.* American Principles Project (available as a free download at https://americanprinciplesproject.org/economics/new-george-gilder-book-the-21st-century-case-for-gold-a-new-information-theory-of-money/).

Gilder, George. *Wealth and Poverty.* Regnery Publishing.

Goldhill, David. *Catastrophic Care: Why Everything We Think We Know About Health Care is Wrong.* Vintage.

Goodman, John. *A Better Choice: Healthcare Solutions for America.* Independent Institute.

Hall, Robert E. and Alvin Rabushka. *The Flat Tax.* Hoover Institution Press.

Hazlitt, Henry. *Economics in One Lesson: Fiftieth Anniversary Edition.* Laissez Faire Books.

Laffer, Arthur B. and Stephen Moore. *An Inquiry into the Nature and Causes of the Wealth of States: How Taxes, Energy and Worker Freedom Change Everything.* Wiley.

Lehrman, Lewis E. *Money, Gold, and History*. The Lehrman Institute.

Lewis, Nathan. *Gold: The Monetary Polaris*. Kindle.

Lewis, Nathan. *Gold: The Once and Future Money*. Wiley.

McDonald, Forrest. *Alexander Hamilton: A Biography*. W.W. Norton & Co.

von Mises, Ludwig. *The Theory of Money and Credit*. Skyhorse Publishing.

Paul, Ron. *End the Fed*. Grand Central Publishing.

Pipes, Sally C. *The Cure for Obamacare*. Encounter Books.

Roy, Avik. *The Case Against Obamacare*. Kindle.

Shelton, Judy. *Fixing the Dollar Now: Why U.S. Money Lost Its Integrity and How We Can Restore It*. Atlas Economic Research Foundation.

Smith, Adam. *The Wealth of Nations*. Simon & Brown.

Tamny, John. *Popular Economics: What the Rolling Stones, Downton Abbey, and LeBron James Can Teach You About Economics*. Regnery Publishing.

Turner, Grace-Marie. *Why Obamacare Is Wrong for America*. Broadside Books.

Wanniski, Jude. *The Way the World Works*. Gateway Contemporary.

Index

100% gold-backed system, 145–147
16th Amendment, income taxes and,
    90–91

Affordable Care Act. *See* Patient
    Protection and Affordable Care Act
Albania, abandons flat tax due to
    politics, 78–79
American republic, principles of, 7
American Revival
    implementing flat tax, 164
    overview, 161–162
    reforming federal reserve, 164–165
    repealing Obamacare, 162–164
assets, expensing vs. depreciating, 66
Atlas, Scott, 35
Axelrod, David, 18

banks
    central. *See* central bank
    easing hyperregulation of, 129
    Fed regulation of, 120
Basel III regulatory standards, 127,
    129–130
Basescu, Traian, 77
Bernanke, Ben, 120, 154
Big Government
    flat tax scaling back, 60
    gold standard and, 139
Birman, Eugene, 75
Bitcoin, 149
bonds
    central bank purchasing to stimulate
        economy, 120–121
    impact of flat tax on tax-free municipal
        bonds, 101
Bretton Woods, 108, 151, 157
Bulgaria, economic growth and flat tax
    in, 78
bureaucracies. *See also* government costly
    bureaucracy needed for Fair Tax, 86
    crushing efficiency of financial system
        and restricting cash flows, 127–129
    gold standard taking decision making
        out of hands of, 139–140
    Keynesian premise of omnipotence
        of, 125
    liability of central planners,
        109–110
Burns, Arthur, 138
Bush, Jeb, 81–82

capital. *See also* investment
    Estonia as magnet for, 74–75
    Fed interference in capital markets,
        127–128
    flat tax attracting foreign capital,
        67
capital gains
    cuts in capital gains taxation increases
        employment, 99
    cuts in capital gains taxation increases
        revenue, 98–99
    eliminating double taxation, 65
    rationale for lower taxes on, 55
Carson, Dr. Ben, 82
Catastrophic Care: Why Everything
    We Think We Know about
    Health Care is Wrong (Goldhill), 12
CDHPs (consumer-directed health
    plans), 20–21
central bank
    compared with currency board,
        146–147
    gold standard in regulation of interest
        rates, 137–138
    lacking accountability, 126
    as lender of last resort under gold
        standard, 150
    purchasing bonds to stimulate
        economy, 120–121
    Quantitative Easing (QE) program. *See*
        Quantitative Easing (QE)
    role in full employment, 124
    role under gold standard, 140
    scaling back role of Fed, 131
central planners. *See also* Federal Reserve
    System
    liability of, 109–110
    reforming federal reserve, 164
"Certificate-of-Need" laws, regulations
    limiting hospital construction,
        18–19
CFPB (Consumer Financial Protection
    Bureau), 128
charitable giving, impact of flat tax on,
    95–97
children, tax exemption for, 62
China
    alternative economic models for, 73
    challenge to U.S. power, 2
Christie, Chris, 82
classical gold standard, 141–143

About the Authors

Steve Forbes is Chairman and Editor-in-Chief of Forbes Media.

The company encompasses *ForbesLife*, *Forbes Europe*, *Forbes Asia* and Forbes licensee editions published in over 37 countries. The company also publishes a number of investment newsletters.

Forbes.com reaches nearly 70 million users each month.

The company's flagship publication, *Forbes*, is the nation's leading business magazine, with a circulation of more than 900,000.

A widely respected economic prognosticator, Mr. Forbes is the only writer to have won the highly prestigious Crystal Owl Award four times. The prize was formerly given by U.S. Steel Corporation to the financial journalist whose economic forecasts for the coming year proved most accurate.

In both 1996 and 2000, Mr. Forbes campaigned vigorously for the Republican nomination for the presidency. Key to his platform were a flat tax, medical savings accounts, a new Social Security system for working Americans, parental choice of schools for their children, term limits and a strong national defense. Mr. Forbes continues to energetically promote this agenda.

Mr. Forbes' book, *Money: How the Destruction of the Dollar Threatens the Global Economy—and What We Can Do About It*, co-authored by Elizabeth Ames (McGraw-Hill), was published in June 2014 and received the coveted Leonard E. Read Book Award.

His other books include *Freedom Manifesto: Why Free Markets are Moral and Big Government Isn't*, co-authored by Elizabeth Ames (Crown Business, August 2012); *How Capitalism Will Save Us: Why Free People and Free Markets Are the Best Answer in Today's Economy*, co-authored by Elizabeth Ames (Crown Business, November 2009);

and *Power Ambition Glory: The Stunning Parallels between Great Leaders of the Ancient World and Today . . . and the Lessons You Can Learn*, co-authored by John Prevas (Crown Business, June 2009). He also wrote: *Flat Tax Revolution: Using a Postcard to Abolish the IRS* (Regnery, 2005); and *A New Birth of Freedom* (Regnery, 1999), a book of bold ideas for the new millennium.

In 1985, President Reagan names Mr. Forbes Chairman of the bi-partisan Board for International Broadcasting (BIB). In this position, he oversaw the operations of Radio Free Europe and Radio Liberty. Broadcasting behind the Iron Curtain, Radio Free Europe and Radio Liberty were praised by Poland's Lech Walesa as being critical to the struggle against communism. Mr. Forbes was reappointed to his post by President George H. W. Bush and served until 1993.

Steve Forbes was born on July 18, 1947, in Morristown, New Jersey. He received a B.A. in history from Princeton in 1970.

Elizabeth Ames has co-authored three previous books with Steve Forbes: *MONEY: How The Destruction of the Dollar Threatens The Global Economy—And What We Can Do About It* (McGraw Hill, 2014); *Freedom Manifesto: Why Free Markets Are Moral and Big Government Isn't* (Crown Business, 2012), in addition to the *Wall Street Journal* bestseller, *How Capitalism Will Save Us: Why Free People and Free Markets Are The Best Answer In Today's Economy* (Crown Business, 2009*)*.

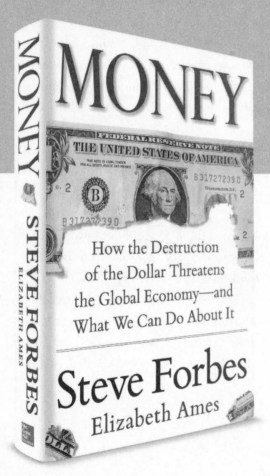